ALABAMA
AND THE
CIVIL WAR

A History & Guide

R O B E R T   C .   J O N E S

THE
History
PRESS

Published by The History Press
Charleston, SC
www.historypress.net

First published 2017

Manufactured in the United States

ISBN 9781625858832

Library of Congress Control Number: 2017931803

Contents

Introduction

In September 2014, I was speaking in Ashville, Alabama, to the St. Clair SCV Camp 308. My book *A Guide to the Civil War in Georgia* was on sale at my lecture venue, and I remember someone in the audience telling me, "You ought to publish *A Guide to the Civil War in Alabama*." I let the idea percolate for several months. After all, there *were* some interesting aspects to the Civil War in Alabama. Union raids into northern Alabama (including one that was linked with the "Great Locomotive Chase" in Georgia); Abel Streight's abortive raid through northern Alabama toward Rome, Georgia; the huge manufacturing infrastructure in central Alabama, Selma, Shelby, Tallassee and other locations; Wilson's Raid; the Battle of Mobile Bay; Canby's attacks at Spanish Fort and Fort Blakeley…well, I guess there is plenty to write about.

There's also a number of important Civil War figures who were native Alabamians, made Alabama their adoptive home or were especially important in the Civil War action in Alabama. Major General Joseph Wheeler and John "the Gallant" Pelham were native Alabamians. Captain Raphael Semmes, Catesby ap Roger Jones, John Washington Inzer, William Lowndes Yancey and Brigadier General Josiah Gorgas made Alabama their adoptive home. And Major General Nathan Bedford Forrest, Major General James Wilson, Major General Edward Canby and Major General Ormsby Mitchel all made their marks on Alabama during the Civil War.

Alabama was important to the Confederate war effort in other ways, too. About 82,500 Alabamians would serve the Confederacy during the war. Alabama's iron furnaces produced 70 percent of the iron supply for the Confederate war effort.[1] It is no wonder that Alabama would be on the receiving end of a two-prong attack in 1865 (by Canby and Wilson). During Wilson's Raid, most of the iron furnaces and arms manufacturing sites were destroyed. Some of them (Brierfield/Bibb and Shelby) would be reconstituted after the war. Other sites (Janney, Tallassee and Selma) would lie silent forever after their destruction.

As this is a guide to the Civil War in Alabama, I am interested not only in presenting history but also a "what is left there today" perspective. I'm not much for the "150 years ago today, this parking lot was the site of a Union attack" school of writing. I'm interested in places that actually have something to see from the war *today*. You'll look in vain for the Battle of Selma or the Battle of Decatur (although there are interpretive signs at both locations). However, the battlefields/forts at Blakeley and Fort McDermott, Fort Gaines and Fort Morgan are reasonably intact.

The following comes from the *Updates to the Civil War Sites Advisory Commission Report on the Nation's Civil War Battlefields: State of Alabama* (National Park Service, 2011). Note that they say in a more formal way what I just described. The only classification that I disagree with a bit is listing Spanish Fort as "landscape and terrain have been altered beyond recognition." While this is true given that the overall battlefield in the modern-day city of Spanish Fort, in April 2015, the carefully cleared and interpreted Fort McDermott joined the ranks of preserved battlefields in the United States.

Condition	Battlefield(s)
Land use is little changed	none
Portions of the landscape have been altered, but most essential features remain	Day's Gap, Fort Blakeley, Mobile Bay
Much of the landscape has been altered and fragmented, leaving some essential features	Athens
Landscape and terrain have been altered beyond recognition	Decatur, Selma, Spanish Fort[2]

Like in most of my recent books, I try to let the participants in the events discussed herein speak for themselves as much as possible. Thanks to sources such as Google Books, Project Gutenberg, the Library of Congress's "Historic Newspapers" and various universities, more and more original source material is being made available online.

Note: A word on spelling: the town of Blakeley is generally spelled with a second *e*. In Union dispatches, Fort Blakeley was spelled without the second *e*. I've maintained that convention throughout this book, using the second *e* except when quoting Union dispatches.

Chapter 1

Key Players

NATHAN BEDFORD FORREST

Nathan Bedford Forrest is perhaps the most controversial general of the Civil War, at least on the Confederate side. He is also probably the greatest cavalry officer in the history of the United States.

Although a wealthy planter before the war, Forrest enlisted as a private in the Confederate army in 1861. He used his own money to outfit his regiment with horses and supplies. He was quickly made a lieutenant colonel.

Nathan Bedford Forrest. *Courtesy of the Library of Congress.*

At the Battle of Fort Donelson, in February 1862, Forrest led almost four thousand troops across the Cumberland River to safety, escaping a siege by Ulysses S. Grant. Shortly after Donelson, Forrest helped evacuate machinery important to Southern manufacturing from Nashville.

On July 13, 1862, Forrest defeated Union general Thomas Crittenden at the First Battle of Murfreesboro. Shortly after, Forrest led two thousand men on a series of raids that disrupted Grant's communication lines during the Vicksburg Campaign.

In April 1863, Forrest was sent to northern Alabama and western Georgia to counter an attack by Union cavalry under Colonel Abel Streight. After pursuing Streight for more than two weeks, Forrest defeated him at Cedar Bluff, Alabama. And during the Battle of Chickamauga, Forrest pursued the retreating army of Rosecrans, capturing several hundred prisoners.

On April 12, 1864, Forrest attacked Fort Pillow near the Mississippi River in western Tennessee. Many black Union troops were killed in the battle, and Forrest was later accused of either ordering a massacre or turning a blind eye to a massacre. Colonel Thomas Jordan, who had recruited Rose Greenhow as a spy back in 1861, wrote *The Campaigns of Lieut.-Gen. N.B. Forrest, and of Forrest's Cavalry* in 1868. Following are some excerpts from his description of the fall of Fort Pillow:

> *It should be remembered that the entrance of the Confederates into the work had been achieved by an impetuous rush over the parapet by each individual, and therefore, for some moments afterward, there was necessarily a general confusion and tumult, in fact, a dissolution of all organizations. Accordingly, as always happens in places taken by storm, unquestionably some whites, as well as negroes, who had thrown down their arms, and besought quarter, were shot under that* insania belli *which invariably rages on such occasions. Nor must it be forgotten that there was no surrender of the place at all. When the Confederates swarmed over the trenches that had been held defiantly for some eight hours in the face of numbers so manifestly superior, the garrison did not yield; did not lay down their arms, nor draw down their flag; but with a lamentable fatuity, the mass of them, with arms still in their hands, fled toward another position in which they were promised relief, and while on the way thither, returned the fire of their pursuers, it is true, not as a mass, but in instances so numerous as to render inevitable a fire upon their whole body, even had it not been the necessary consequence of their efforts to escape capture, whether with arms in their hands or not.*

In the mean time, or as soon as he could reach the scene, Forrest, riding into the work, assisted by Captain John Overton, lowered the flag; and immediately both he, General Chalmers, and other officers interfered so energetically to stop the firing that it ceased speedily; ceased within fifteen minutes from the time that the signal for the termination of the truce was given, and all allegations to the contrary are mere malicious inventions, started, nurtured, and accredited at a time, and through a sentiment of strong sectional animosity. The first order, indeed, now issued by General Forrest, was to collect and secure the prisoners from possible injury, while details were made from them for the burial of the Federal dead.....General Forrest ordered the Federal dead to be buried in the trenches of the work, the officers to be interred separately from their men...

[Here Jordan quotes Captain Goodman:] *"On the following morning, (the 13th), a detail was sent to the Fort to collect and remove the remaining arms, and to bury such of the dead as might have been overlooked on the day before. They had been at work but a short time when a gunboat (the* Silver Cloud*) came up and began to shell them. As this became annoying, the officer commanding the detail ordered the tents which were still standing in the Fort to be burned, intending to abandon the place. In doing this, the bodies of some negroes who had been killed in the tents, on the day before, were somewhat burned; and this probably gave rise to the horrible stories about burning wounded prisoners which were afterward invented and circulated."*[3]

On June 10, 1864, Forrest defeated Union general Samuel Sturgis at the Battle of Brice's Crossroads (Mississippi). Although outnumbered almost three to one, Forrest won a resounding victory, suffering 492 casualties to the Union's 2,000 plus.

Thomas Jordan wrote about the results of the Battle of Brice's Crossroads, as well as the skill of Forrest in conducting the battle in 1868:

The enemy began their retreat about four p.m. on the 10th, and by five p.m. on the 11th they had been driven, with heavy loss, in frequent collisions with the Confederates, quite fifty-eight miles, with the loss also of nineteen pieces of artillery, twenty-one caissons, over two hundred wagons, and thirty ambulances, with parts of their teams and large quantities of subsistence, ammunition, and other materiel of war. More than 2000 officers and men, including the wounded, were taken prisoners; and 1900 of their dead were left upon the field or by the wayside, between the battlefield and Ripley.

Seldom, almost never, was an army more completely beaten and dispersed than that of Sturgis on this occasion; beaten too, as has been seen, by a force of fighting men at no time exceeding 3200 men, that is to say, little over one third of the Federal army. The Confederate losses were severe, at least 140 officers and men killed, and nearly 500 were wounded....

    In this battle the genuine military capacity of General Forrest would seem to have been demonstrated. It has been thought and asserted by many that his successes were largely due to uncommon good fortune, coupled with audacity; but it must be apparent that this brilliant victory was won by his prompt comprehension of the situation on the morning of the 10th June, and his recognition of the possibility of taking his adversary at the sore disadvantage of being attacked while his column was extended in a long line, moving over the narrow roads of that densely wooded region. Seeing his advantage at its right value, he planned and executed with equal celerity; and never did soldiers fight, we repeat, with greater tenacity or intrepidity than those he led that day.[4]

Things went downhill after Brice's Crossroads, as Forrest served under John Bell Hood's command in the Franklin-Nashville Campaign. He was defeated by Major General James Wilson at the Battle of Selma on April 2, 1865. Forrest surrendered in May 1865.

After the war, Forrest helped start the Ku Klux Klan. He eventually quit the Klan because it was too violent for his liking.

Forrest probably didn't say that the essence of battle was to "git thar fustest with the mostest." But it does describe his theories about the importance of mobile warfare. World War I generals should have studied Forrest's battle tactics.

July 13 is "Nathan Bedford Forrest Day" in Tennessee.

Date	Event(s)
July 13, 1821	Forrest is born in Chapel Hill, Tennessee.
1841	Goes into business in Hernando, Mississippi, with his uncle Jonathan Forrest.
1845	After the Matlock brothers kill his uncle, Forrest kills two of them and wounds two others.
1858	Elected as a Memphis alderman.

Date	Event(s)
1861	Is one of the richest men in the South, as a plantation owner and slave trader.
July 14, 1861	Joins the Tennessee Mounted Rifles as a private. In time, Forrest would outfit the company with horses and other equipment. He was quickly promoted to lieutenant colonel.
October 1861	Becomes regimental commander of "Forrest's Cavalry Corps."
February 1862	At the Battle of Fort Donelson, Forrest leads four thousand men out of the besieged fort to escape.
April 6–April 7, 1862	Battle of Shiloh takes place. Forrest is shot in the spine after charging a Union regiment by himself (Battle of Fallen Timbers, April 8, 1862).
July 13, 1862	First Battle of Murfreesboro.
July 1862	Promoted to brigadier general.
December 1862	Braxton Bragg reassigns Forrest's brigade and gives Forrest a new brigade of two thousand inexperienced and (mostly) unarmed troops.
1863	Raids in the Vicksburg area.
May 3, 1863	Defeats Colonel Abel Streight at Cedar Bluff, Alabama; 1,500 Union prisoners taken.
June 14, 1863	Gets into a fight with his artillery commander, Lieutenant A. Wills Gould. Gould shoots Forrest in the hip, and Forrest stabs him to death.
September 19–September 20, 1863	Battle of Chickamauga. Forrest aggressively pursues the retreating Union army toward Chattanooga, capturing hundreds. After the battle, he criticizes Braxton Bragg for not pursuing more aggressively, saying, "What does he fight battles for?"
December 4, 1863	Promoted to major general; earlier, Forrest had been reassigned to the Mississippi by Jefferson Davis, after Forrest threatened to kill Braxton Bragg.

Date	Event(s)
April 12, 1864	Attack on Fort Pillow, located on the Mississippi at Henning, Tennessee. Forrest is later accused of a massacre of black troops who had tried to surrender.
June 10, 1864	Huge victory at the Battle of Brice's Crossroads (Lee County, Mississippi) against Union brigadier general Samuel D. Sturgis.
July 14–15, 1864	Defeated and wounded at the Battle of Tupelo.
August 21, 1864	Raids supply lines in Memphis.
October 3, 1864	Raids Union supply depot at Johnsonville, Tennessee.
November 30, 1864	Fights under John Bell Hood at the disastrous Battle of Franklin, Tennessee.
December 5, 1864	Union victory at the Third Battle of Murfreesboro.
December 15–16, 1864	Crushing Union victory at Nashville; Forrest fights a successful rear-guard action and is promoted to lieutenant general.
December 25, 1864	Part of Forrest's command is surprised and captured in Verona, Mississippi.
March–April 1865	Defeated by Brigadier General James H. Wilson during Wilson's Raid of Alabama at Ebenezer Church and Selma.
May 9, 1865	Farewell address at Gainesville, Alabama.
1866–69	Joins the Ku Klux Klan and possibly becomes grand wizard.
1869	Disbands the Klan.
May 11, 1870	Forrest City, Arkansas, is incorporated.

Date	Event(s)
1870s	President of the Marion and Memphis Railroad (Selma, Alabama), which eventually goes bankrupt.
1873	Offers his service to William Tecumseh Sherman in case of a war with Spain; Sherman replies and says it would be an honor to serve with Forrest.
1875	Gives a speech to the Independent Order of Pole-Bearers Association, an organization of black southerners.
October 29, 1877	Dies in Memphis, Tennessee, of diabetes.
1918	A *New York Times* article quotes Forrest as saying, "Ma'am, I got there first with the most men."
December 1929	Nathan Bedford Forrest State Park is established in Tennessee.
June 13, 1943	Brigadier General Nathan Bedford Forrest III is killed in a bombing run over Germany. He is awarded the Distinguished Service Cross posthumously.

Josiah Gorgas

I have always asserted that you, General Gorgas, organized the only successful Military Bureau during our National existence, and this is the more surprising, as you had less foundation to go on than any other.
—General Braxton Bragg

He created the Ordnance Department out of nothing.
—General Joseph E. Johnston[5]

Brigadier General Josiah Gorgas created the Confederate munitions industry out of practically nothing in his time as chief of ordnance for the Confederacy. Prior to the war, he had served in arsenals including Watervliet Arsenal (Troy, New York), Detroit Arsenal, Mount Vernon Arsenal (north of Mobile, Alabama) and Frankford Arsenal (Philadelphia, Pennsylvania). He also established a relationship with the Tredegar Iron Company in Richmond while he was assigned to Fort Monroe. When the Civil War broke out in 1861, Gorgas was the obvious choice to serve as chief of ordnance for the Confederacy.

Gorgas helped establish the Confederate Powder Works at Augusta, Georgia, and moved the massive Mount Vernon Arsenal from near Mobile, Alabama, to safer quarters in Selma. In 1864, he moved the Richmond Carbine Factory from Richmond to Tallassee, Alabama, also for safety reasons. He negotiated with European arms manufacturers, especially in England, to procure arms for the Confederacy (that often had to be brought in via blockade runners).

In 1864, on the third anniversary of his appointment as chief of ordnance for the Confederacy, Gorgas looked back on his accomplishments in his journal:

> *April 8th. It is three years ago today since I took charge of the Ordnance Department of the Confederate States, at Montgomery—three years of constant work and application. I have succeeded beyond my utmost expectations. From being the worst supplied of the Bureaus of the War Department it is now the best. Large arsenals have been organized at Richmond, Fayetteville, Augusta, Charleston, Columbus, Macon, Atlanta and Selma, and smaller ones at Danville, Lynchburgh and Montgomery, besides other establishments. A superb powder mill has been built at Augusta, the credit of which is due to Col. G.W. Rains. Lead smelting works were established by me at Petersburgh [Petersburg], and turned over to the Nitre and Mining Bureau, when that Bureau was at my request separated from mine. A cannon foundry established at Macon for heavy guns, and bronze foundries at Macon, Columbus, Ga., and at Augusta; a foundry for shot and shell at Salisbury, N.C.; a large shop for leather work at Clarksville, Va.; besides the Armories here and at Fayetteville, a manufactory of carbines has been built up here; a rifle factory at Ashville (transferred to Columbia, S.C.); a new and very large armory at Macon, including a pistol factory, built up under contract here and sent to Atlanta, and thence transferred under purchase to Macon; a second pistol factory at Columbus, Ga.; All of these have required incessant toil and attention, but have borne such fruit as relieves the country from fear of want in these respects. Where three years ago we were not making a gun, a pistol nor a sabre, no shot nor shell (except at the Tredegar Works)—a pound of powder—we now make all these in quantities to meet the demands of our large armies. In looking over all this I feel that my three years of labor have not been passed in vain.*[6]

By May 1865, Gorgas (like other Confederate leaders stationed in Richmond) was on the run, heading back to Alabama via Georgia. He noted in a diary entry from 1865:

> *Thursday, May 4. We are discussing the propriety of setting out again on our progress southward and will probably leave on Saturday. I desire to set forward to Alabama, as my adopted State, before again coming under the control of the authority of the U.S. Govt. We took tea at Mrs. Jas. Aiken's last night and are to dine with Mr. Taft today.*
>
> *The calamity which has fallen upon us in the total destruction of our government is of a character so overwhelming that I am as yet unable to comprehend it. I am as one walking in a dream, and expecting to awake. I cannot see its consequences nor shape my own course, but am just moving along until I can see my way at some future day. It is marvelous that a people that a month ago had money, armies, and the attributes of a nation should today be no more, and that we live, breathe, move, talk as before—will it be so when the soul leaves the body behind it?*[7]

After the war, in 1866, the Canebrake Company, under the leadership of Gorgas, purchased the Bibb County Iron Company for $45,000 and renamed it Brierfield Coal and Iron Company. The venture was ultimately not successful. Again, from Gorgas's diary:

> *Briarfield, January 20, 1866. I reached here yesterday to take up my permanent residence here. The company of which I am a member bought this property on the 9th of Jany. for $45,000, and I am to manage it for them. The members of the Co. are messrs Lyon, Collins, Frank griffin, Mrs. Wynne, Dr. Whitfield & Dr. Bowder of Demopolis, shares of $10,000 each and Mrs. Bruce half a share, and Col. Crawford, Wm. H. Ross of Mobile & myself, one share each making $95,000 in all. $5,000 are held in reserve. I expect to spend $30,000 in machinery & repairs, & shall then have $25,000 to start with. The company can readily be increased if necessary.*[8]

In 1878, Gorgas became president of the University of Alabama at Tuscaloosa, a position that he relinquished when he had a stroke one year later. He then became librarian of the university, a position that his wife assumed after his death in 1883.

Date	Event(s)
July 1, 1818	Gorgas is Born in Running Pumps, Dauphin County, Pennsylvania.
1841	Graduates from West Point (sixth in his class); he serves at the Watervliet Arsenal (Troy, New York) and at the Detroit Arsenal.
1847–48	Serves in the Mexican-American War as a member of the ordnance staff of General Winfield Scott in Veracruz; he contracts yellow fever.
after the Mexican-American War	Returns to Watervliet Arsenal.
November 1851	Begins serving at Fort Monroe in Virginia and interacts with the Tredegar Iron Company.
1853	Marries Amelia Gayle. She was the daughter of former Alabama governor John Gayle. She and Josiah would have six children. William C. Gorgas would one day be U.S. Army surgeon general. Serves at the Mount Vernon Arsenal (north of Mobile, Alabama).
1855	Is promoted to the rank of captain.
March 21, 1861	Resigns from the U.S. Army and relinquishes command of the Frankford Arsenal in Philadelphia, Pennsylvania.
April 8, 1861	Is made chief of ordnance for the Confederacy; he had been earlier promoted to major.
summer 1861	Begins expanding the Augusta Armory in Georgia.
September 1861	Establishes the Confederate powder mill at Augusta, Georgia.
1862	After the fall of New Orleans, Gorgas moves the massive Mount Vernon Arsenal to Selma.

Date	Event(s)
summer 1864	Moves Richmond Carbine Factory from Richmond to the Tallassee Manufacturing Company.
November 10, 1864	Is promoted to brigadier general.
1866–69	Runs the Brierfield Iron Works, near Montevallo, Alabama.
1869	Headmaster at the University of the South in Sewanee, Tennessee.
1878	President of the University of Alabama at Tuscaloosa.
February 23, 1879	Suffers massive stroke.
July 1879	Resigns as president but is given the job of university librarian. His wife assumes this position after his death in 1883.
May 15, 1883	Dies in Tuscaloosa, Alabama.
1944	The Gorgas House at the University of Alabama, once the home of Gorgas and his family, becomes a memorial.

JULIET ANN OPIE HOPKINS

Juliet Ann Opie Hopkins and her husband started three military hospitals in Richmond in 1861–62 for Alabama soldiers (in those days, each state had to care for its own wounded). The Alabama legislature made Juliet hospital superintendent in all three hospitals. Later, in 1864, she served as the administrator of the military hospital at Camp Watts in Tuskegee, Alabama.

Known for her bravery in attending to the wounded on the battlefield, she was wounded herself while rescuing casualties at the Battle of Seven Pines. Juliet was sometimes referred to as the "Florence Nightingale of the South." A nurse named Fannie Beers published her memoirs in 1888 and described an incident in Richmond that shows how quickly and efficiently Juliet Hopkins managed emergencies concerning wounded Alabamian troops:

One morning, just as I had arrived there and was preparing to begin my daily duties, a carriage stopped at the door, from which Mrs. Judge Hopkins descended, and, hastily entering the hospital, announced to the ladies that she had "come for Mrs. Beers." They strongly demurred, and I felt at first great hesitation in obeying so hasty a summons. But Mrs. Hopkins was very much in earnest. "Indeed, you must come," said she, "for I have great need of you. A large number of sick and wounded Alabamians will arrive this morning. I have found a place to put them, but someone must be there to prepare for their accommodation, to receive hospital supplies, and direct their arrangement, while I make purchases and attend to other matters. Come," holding out both hands towards me; "no hireling can fill the place. Come, now, with me: we have no time to lose." I hesitated no longer, but entered the carriage. We were at once driven downtown, stopping to order cots, mattresses, etc., then to...an immense tobacco factory, owned by Messrs. Turpin & Yarborough.

Arrived here, a pitiful sight met our eyes. Perhaps fifty sick men had arrived unexpectedly, and were sitting or lying about in every conceivable position expressive of feebleness, extreme illness, utter exhaustion. Mr. Yarborough, having given up the keys to Mrs. Hopkins, was impatiently pacing in and out among the prostrate men. Coming upon this scene, both Mrs. Hopkins and myself at once realized all that lay before us, and braced our nerves to meet the emergency.

The men were soon under shelter, but no beds, had yet arrived. Mrs. Hopkins led me into the factory, introduced me to Dr. Clark, who had come to take charge as surgeon, and placed me under him at the head of affairs as her deputy. A corps of nurses, hastily summoned, were ordered to report to me.

Meantime immense boxes arrived from the depot, sent by the people of Alabama. These contained pillows, comforts, sheets, as well as wines, cordials, and every delicacy for the sick, also quantities of shirts, drawers, and socks, old and new. The boxes were wrenched open, pillows placed quickly under the heads of the sickest, and cordials administered. As the beds came in they were placed, made up, and the worst cases first, others afterward, were transferred to them, until all were lying comfortably between clean sheets and clad in clean shirts and drawers. There was no lack of food, both substantial and of a kind proper for the very sick.[9]

The $0.25 piece and the $50 bill issued by Alabama during the war used her image. Juliet died on May 9, 1890, and was buried at Arlington National Cemetery.

Date	Event(s)
May 7, 1818	Hopkins is born in Jefferson County, Virginia.
1837	Marries Commodore Alexander Gordon (d. 1849).
1854	Marries Judge Arthur F. Hopkins (d. 1866).
1861–62	Juliet and her husband finance and start up three military hospitals in Richmond for Alabama soldiers; Juliet is made hospital superintendent of all three hospitals by the Alabama legislature.
July 1, 1862	Wounded at the Battle of Seven Pines while administering to wounded on the battlefield.
1864	Serves as administrator of the military hospital at Camp Watts in Tuskegee, Alabama.
February 22, 1873	Receives a silver service from the Mobile Rifles.
May 9, 1890	Dies in Washington, D.C. Is buried at Arlington National Cemetery at the grave site of her niece's husband, Union general Romeyn Beck Ayers.

JOHN WASHINGTON INZER

Lieutenant-Colonel Inzer behaved with conspicuous gallantry during the engagement, and rendered much valuable aid by words and example, in causing the men to charge with enthusiasm, and in reforming the regiment.[10]
—*Colonel Bushrod Jones, in his report of the Battle of Chickamauga,*
September 19, 1863

John Washington Inzer was born in Gwinnett County, Georgia, in 1834 but moved to St. Clair County, Alabama, with his family in 1853. From 1855 to the start of the Civil War, Inzer worked as a lawyer and probate judge.

In 1861, Inzer represented St. Clair County at the Secession Convention. Inzer initially voted against secession but later voted for it in a gesture for unity.

Although in poor health, he joined the Confederate army as a private in the 9th Alabama Infantry Battalion. He would rise to the rank of lieutenant colonel

John Washington Inzer.

by 1863. He fought in numerous battles, including at Shiloh, Corinth, Chickamauga, Lookout Mountain and Missionary Ridge, where he was captured. Inzer described his capture in a diary he wrote while in prison:

Just before sunrise on November 25th, 1863, we were in line of battle on Missionary Ridge near Breckinridge headquarters....

We then commenced to fight in earnest. Before a great while, I discovered the enemy was flanking us on the left. He was coming up a hollow some 100 yards from the left of our regiments, moving by the flank....I then attempted to rally my right and move by the left flank across the hollow for the purpose of checking this flanking movement of the enemy. After repeated efforts, succeeded only partially in doing what I desired to do. In a few minutes more, the balance of the Brigade commenced giving away. Moving up the ridge on top, I never worked so hard in my life as I did that morning to rally my command. They may have heard the command "Retreat" given. I never did hear an order to fall back. I stood there until every man left me begging them to come back and fight the enemy. I remained here until the men who had been with me were 100 or 150 yards from me—near where Col. Holtzclaw was sitting on his horde, understood they were at the breast-works on the right of the regiment. Seeing my men all gone, I moved up to there. Holtzclaw was sitting on his horse. I went to him and begged him to rally the men. I told him most of the men knew him and I believed he could rally them at a point some 200 yards in our rear. Then asked him to send one of his staff. I was on foot. He declined to do so. In a few minutes more he told me the order was to face back in four ranks (column of squads). This was the first order I ever heard to face back. After the above conversation, the Colonel put spurs to his horse and that was the last I ever saw of him.

I then moved back on the ridge in the direction of Gen. Breckinridge's Quarters, some 300 yards. Saw the men filing to the right down the ridge through a field. Here Col. Jones and Major Thornton passed me—both on the Colonel's mare. I turned down the hill trying to get the men on my left to follow me. After getting some 100 yards down the ridge, was fired into several times from my left. The hog-weeds were so high and thick, I could not see anyone. Believing this to be our friends, I hollowed several times to stop the fire, but without effect. Turned—saw several of my officers and men on top of the ridge waving their hats. Thought they were hollowing to the men on my left to stop shooting into us. There being so much noise and confusion, I could not hear what they said. Being anxious to stop the firing, I went back to where my officers were, but to my sorrow, saw when I got there that they had surrendered, surrounded by thousands of the enemy—seeing further resistance useless, I stuck my sword in the ground and became a prisoner. A large number of the officers and men of the 32-36-38 and 58 Ala. regiments were captured at and near said point. This was about sun set. Surrendered to the Second Ohio. We were well treated.[11]

After the war, he served in numerous capacities in the community, including as probate judge, state senator, as a member of the Alabama Constitutional Convention, as trustee of Howard College (Samford University), as trustee of the Alabama Insane Hospital and as judge of the Sixteenth Judicial Circuit. When he died in 1928, he was the "Grand Old Man" of Alabama.

In 1866, Judge Inzer purchased a house in Ashville. In July 1987, that house (now known as the Inzer House) and its contents were deeded by Inzer descendants to the St. Clair Camp 308 SCV, which maintains it today as a museum and meeting place. I've given lectures in that house on numerous occasions.

Date	Event(s)
January 9, 1834	Inzer is born in Gwinnett County, Georgia.
1853	Family moves to St. Clair County, Alabama.
May 1855	Admitted to the bar in Talladega.
1856	Sets up law practice in Ashville.
1859	Probate judge, St. Clair County.

Date	Event(s)
1861	Represents St. Clair County at the Secession Convention; Inzer initially votes against secession but later votes for it in a gesture for unity. Although in poor health, he joins Confederate army as a private in the 9th Alabama Infantry Battalion.
1862	Transfers to 18th Infantry.
February 1863	Becomes captain and then major of 9th Alabama Infantry.
July 1863	9th Alabama Infantry becomes 58th Alabama Infantry Regiment, with Inzer later receiving the rank of lieutenant colonel (August 12, 1863).
September 19–20, 1863	Battle of Chickamauga.
November 25, 1863	Captured at Battle of Missionary Ridge.
1863–65	Imprisoned at Johnson's Island.
June 27, 1865	Released from Johnson's Island.
1866	Marries Miss Sallie E. Pope; they will have two daughters and one son. Purchases today's Inzer House in Ashville. Elected probate judge.
1867	Removed as probate judge by military authorities.
1874	Elected to Alabama Senate.
1875	Elected to Constitutional Convention.
1877	Appointed as trustee of Howard College (Samford University).
1878–1900	Trustee of the Alabama Insane Hospital.
1890	Elected to state Senate.

Date	Event(s)
May 31, 1906	Inzer donates the flag of the 58th Alabama Infantry Regiment to the Alabama Department of Archives and History.
1907–8	Judge of the Sixteenth Judicial Circuit.
January 2, 1928	Dies and is buried at the Ashville Cemetery—the "Grand Old Man" of Alabama.
July 1987	Inzer House and contents deeded by Inzer descendants to the St. Clair Camp 308 SCV.

CATESBY AP ROGER JONES

The services which you are rendering at Selma are regarded by this Department as more important to the Country than any which you could otherwise perform in the Navy, and not less valuable to its best interests than those which are being rendered by any other Naval officer.[12]

—S.R. Mallory, September 16, 1864

Catesby ap Roger Jones.

Although born in Virginia, Commander Catesby ap[13] Roger Jones was assigned to Alabama in 1863 and remained there after the war. He is best known for captaining the CSS *Virginia* (*Merrimack*) against the USS *Monitor* on March 9, 1862, at Hampton Roads, Virginia.

In 1836, Jones was appointed midshipman, U.S. Navy, and served under his uncle Thomas ap Catesby Jones. He was promoted to lieutenant in 1849. After his promotion, he would go on to study ordnance under

Admiral John Dahlgren, inventor of the Dahlgren gun. In 1856, he was named ordnance officer on the steam frigate, which would soon be fitted with Dahlgren guns—Jones was one of the few people in the country who understood how the new guns operated.

By June 1861, he was a lieutenant in the Confederate navy. His first assignment in 1861–62 was to turn the captured USS *Merrimack* into an ironclad. He was named the executive officer on the newly christened CSS *Virginia*. On March 8–9, 1862, when Captain Franklin Buchanan was wounded, Jones assumed command of the *Merrimack* (CSS *Virginia*), acting as captain when the *Merrimack* had its epic battle with the USS *Monitor* in Hampton Roads, Virginia.

From July 1862 to February 4, 1863, he served as the commander of the CSS *Chattahoochee*. He comes into our story in this book when he was promoted to commander and sent to Selma to run the Selma Ordnance and Naval Foundry on April 29, 1863. He would maintain this post until the end of the war. He was a key part in building up the Selma Ordnance and Naval Foundry into the behemoth it was by the end of the war.

He died on June 20, 1877, in Selma, when he got caught in the crossfire between his son and another man.

Date	Event(s)
April 15, 1821	Jones is born in Fairfield, Virginia.
1836	Appointed midshipman, U.S. Navy, under his uncle Thomas ap Catesby Jones.
1849	Promoted to lieutenant.
1856	Ordnance officer on the steam frigate USS *Merrimack*, which would soon be fitted with Dahlgren guns.
April 1861	Resigns from the U.S. Navy.
June 1861	Lieutenant in the Confederate navy.
1861–62	Involved in turning the USS *Merrimack* into an ironclad; executive officer on CSS *Virginia*.
March 8, 1862–March 9, 1862	Assumes command of the *Merrimack* (CSS *Virginia*) when Captain Franklin Buchanan is wounded; is acting captain when the *Merrimack* meets the USS *Monitor*.

Date	Event(s)
July 1862–February 4, 1863	Commander of the CSS *Chattahoochee*.
April 29, 1863	Promoted to commander and sent to Selma to run the Selma Ordnance and Naval Foundry.
April 2, 1865	Selma falls.
January 20, 1866	Begins service in Peru as a military consultant.
February 28, 1866	Returns to United States.
June 20, 1877	Dies in Selma, Alabama, as collateral damage in a gunfight.

ANDREW B. MOORE

"Andrew B. Moore, war governor of Ala."
Courtesy of the Library of Congress.

Andrew B. Moore was a lawyer, justice of the peace, judge and governor of Alabama (1857–61). It was he who called for the Secession Convention in Montgomery in early 1861 and he who ordered the seizure on January 7, 1861, of the arsenal at Mount Vernon (which was later moved to Selma), as well as Fort Morgan and Fort Gaines at the entrance to Mobile Bay. Note that this occurred several months before the firing on Fort Sumter (April 12–13, 1861) and was considered premature by many people in the Confederacy. He also was involved in the seizure of Federal forts in Pensacola, Florida.

Moore also made improvements in the State of Alabama social

system, including the construction of the Alabama Insane Hospital at Tuscaloosa, the creation of the Institute for the Deaf and Blind at Talladega and the establishment of the Medical College in Mobile.

On December 2, 1861, his successor, Governor John Gill Shorter, was sworn in. Shorter then appointed Moore as a special aide-de-camp for military affairs, especially in northern Alabama.

Date	Event(s)
March 7, 1807	Moore is born near Spartanburg, South Carolina.
1823	Family moves to Perry County, Alabama.
1826–28	Teaches school in Perry County, Alabama.
1833	Admitted to the bar and begins serving as justice of the peace for Perry County.
1837	Marries Mary Goree; they would have three children.
1839	Elected to the Alabama House of Representatives.
1843–45	Speaker of the House, Alabama House of Representatives.
1851	Appointed circuit judge by the governor.
1852	Elected circuit judge.
1857–61	Governor of Alabama.
January 7, 1861	Orders the Alabama state militia to seize the arsenal at Mount Vernon (which was later moved to Selma), as well as Fort Morgan and Fort Gaines at the entrance to Mobile Bay.
early 1861	Sends five hundred militia troops to help Florida capture Federal forts at Pensacola.
February 1861	Supports election of Jefferson Davis as provisional president of the Confederacy.
December 2, 1861	After his successor is sworn in, Governor John Gill Shorter appoints Moore as a special aide-de-camp for military affairs.

Date	Event(s)
May 1865	Imprisoned in Fort Pulaski in Savannah, Georgia.
August 1865	Released from Fort Pulaski because of poor health and returns to his law practice in Marion, Alabama.
April 5, 1873	Dies in Marion, Alabama.

JOHN PELHAM

As soon as the advance of the enemy was discovered through the fog, General Stuart, with his accustomed promptness, moved up a section of his horse artillery, which opened with effect upon his flank and threw upon the gallant Pelham a heavy fire, which he sustained unflinchingly for about two hours.[14]
—Robert E. Lee, Report on the Battle of Fredericksburg

John Pelham is, perhaps, the most famous soldier from Alabama under the rank of general. In 1861, he resigned from West Point a few weeks short of his graduation date and joined the Confederate army. At the Battle of First Manassas (Bull Run), his handling of artillery so impressed J.E.B. Stuart that Stuart recruited him to organize his horse (mobile) artillery.

Pelham would fight in sixty battles, including First and Second Manassas, Antietam, Fredericksburg and Kelly's Ford. In an age when cavalry was used primarily for scouting purposes, Pelham fit in well with Stuart's vision of cavalry as a hit-and-run mechanism. It is sometimes postulated that Pelham defined the very idea of light artillery as a part of an offensive cavalry.

He received the sobriquet "the Gallant Pelham" because of his bravery and effectiveness at the Battle of Fredericksburg, a battle where Stonewall Jackson actually let Pelham position his artillery where Pelham thought best. Lee used the phrase "the Gallant Pelham" in his report on the battle.

At the tender age of twenty-four, Pelham met his death at the Battle of Kelly's Ford. His death is described by the adjutant of the 3rd Cavalry:

At the moment a regiment of Federal cavalry swept down upon us. Pelham's sabre flashed from its sheath in an instant. At that moment his appearance was superb. His cheeks were burning; his bright blue eyes darted lightning, and from his lips, wreathed with a smile of joy, rang, "Forward!" as he cheered on the men. He looked the perfect picture of a hero, as he was. For

"Gallant Pelham" statue at the Jacksonville, Alabama city cemetery. *Author's collection.*

an instant he was standing in his stirrups, his sabre flashing in his grasp; for a moment his clarion voice rang like a bugle that sounds the charge, and then I saw him hurled from his saddle under the tramping hoofs of the horses. With a single bound of my horse I reached him. He lay with his smiling face turned upward; his eyes closed. A shell had burst above him, a fragment of which had struck him on the head. He was gone, and his young blood, sacred to the men of his battery and the entire command, had bathed Virginia's soil.[15]

"Major John C. Pelham of Alburtis Light Artillery and 1st Co. Stuart Horse Virginia Light Artillery Battery in Uniform." *Courtesy of the Library of Congress.*

On March 20, 1863, J.E.B. Stuart commented on Pelham's death in his General Order No. 9:

The major-general commanding approaches with reluctance the painful duty of announcing to the division its irreparable loss in the death of Major John Pelham, commanding the Horse Artillery. He fell mortally wounded in the battle of Kellysville, March 17th, with the battle-cry on his lips, and the light of victory beaming from his eye....His eye had glanced on every battlefield of this army from the First Manassas to the moment of his death, and he was, with a single exception, a brilliant actor in them all. The memory of "the gallant Pelham," his many manly virtues, his noble nature and purity of character, are enshrined as a sacred legacy in the hearts of all who knew him. His record has been bright and spotless, his career brilliant and successful.[16]

At least three poems have been written about him, including one by Cordelia Elizabeth Moore (first below), one by A. Sydney Morton (second below) and one by Larry Maffit Jr. in 1894 (not shown).

"The Gallant Pelham"

Dedicated to the Pelham Chapter, United Daughters Confederacy, Birmingham, Ala.

We honor him, the brave and true,
And written on the scroll of fame,
In living characters today,
Our "Gallant Pelham's" name.

A glorious legacy bequeathed,
By Southern heroes, slain,
But none with brighter lustre shines,
Than "Gallant Pelham's" name.

And memories come to us today,
Of pleasures and of pain,
His early and heroic death,
Leaving a stainless name.

'Tis meet, we honor him, the brave,
Though feel the effort vain,
To add one laurel to the wreath,
Of "Gallant Pelham's" fame.

May our devotion to this work,
Enlist each Southern dame,
And may our children ne'er forget,
Our "Gallant Pelham's" name.[17]

"The Gallant Pelham"

Into the hurtling storm of shell,
Into the gaping mouth of hell,
Pelham, the dauntless, dashed
Out from the meagre line of gray,
Out to the bloody fringe of fray,
Where thousand thunders crashed.

Lashes to straining horses plied,
Cheers of defiance as they ride,
Under the eye of Lee.
Out of the day and into night,
Clouded in smoke they ride to fight,
Glorious sight to see!

Out of the bedlam Freedom speaks,
Hear it in Pelham's Parrot's shrieks.
Pelham!, 'tis bravely done!
In the concentrating, deadly hail;
Daring to die, but not to fail,
Pelham still fights his gun!

What is that sound? 'Tis not a cheer
There, yet again—list! Comrade?, hear!
Hark, 'tis the hymn of France!
Rising, the lofty anthem swells,
Over the din of countless hells,
Freedom defiance chants!

Never was witnessed braver deed,
Bringing of praise its richest meed [reward],
Making a deathless name
"Courage sublime in one so young!"
Words from the heart of Lee he swung,
"Crown of immortal fame!"[18]

Date	Event(s)
September 7, 1838	Pelham is born near Alexandria, Alabama.
July 1, 1856	Appointed to West Point.
1861	Resigns from West Point a few weeks short of his graduation date. Joins the Confederate army under Joseph Johnston as a lieutenant in the artillery.

Date	Event(s)
July 21, 1861	Recruited by J.E.B. Stuart after the Battle of First Manassas (Bull Run) to organize his horse (mobile) artillery.
November 1861	Promoted to captain, in charge of Stuart's horse artillery.
September 17, 1862	Battle of Antietam. By this point, Pelham was chief of artillery for J.E.B. Stuart.
December 11–15, 1862	Battle of Fredericksburg. Lee refers to him as "the Gallant Pelham" in his report of the battle.
March 17, 1863	Leads cavalry charge at Kelly's Ford, where he was mortally wounded.
1863	Receives posthumous promotion to lieutenant colonel from the Confederate Senate.
post–Civil War	Pelham, Alabama, is named.
1881	Pelham, Georgia, is incorporated.
July 1, 1887	Post office in service at Pelham, North Carolina.
1894	Larry Maffit Jr. writes the poem "John Pelham."
1901	A portrait in his honor is hung in Alexandria, Virginia; Major General Joseph Wheeler delivers the address.
1905	Statue is erected to Pelham in Jacksonville, Alabama.
1955	Named to the Alabama Hall of Fame.

EDMUND PETTUS

Edmund Pettus, born near Athens, Alabama, in 1821, was a soldier, lawyer, judge and U.S. senator. As a soldier, he fought in the Mexican-American War, reaching the rank of lieutenant. In the Civil War, he reached the rank of brigadier general and fought with distinction at Stones River, Vicksburg, Missionary Ridge, in the Atlanta Campaign and against Sherman in the Carolinas Campaign.

He was captured three times—at Stones River, Vicksburg and Port Gibson. Twice he returned to service via a prisoner exchange, and once he escaped back to his own lines (Port Gibson).

After the war, he returned to his law practice, and then, in 1877, he became grand dragon of the Alabama Ku Klux Klan. He served for ten years as a U.S. senator from Alabama (1897–1907).

In 1940, the Edmund Pettus Bridge was built in Selma to cross the Alabama River. This was later the site of three civil rights marches in March 1965, the first one culminating in "Bloody Sunday," in which sixty-seven protesters were injured and/or hospitalized.

Efforts to rename the bridge to this date have not been successful.

Date	Event(s)
July 6, 1821	Pettus is born in Limestone County, Alabama (near Athens).
1842	Admitted to the state's bar association.
June 27, 1844	Marries Mary L. Chapman (they would have three children).

Edmund Pettus Bridge in 2015. Selma is on the right side of the picture. *Author's collection.*

Date	Event(s)
1844	Elected solicitor for the Seventh Judicial Circuit of Alabama.
1847–49	Serves as a lieutenant in the Mexican-American War with the Alabama Volunteers.
1855–58	Appointed as a judge in the Seventh Judicial Circuit of Alabama.
1858	Moves to Cahaba, Alabama.
1861	Serves as a Democratic Party delegate to the Secession Convention in Mississippi (his brother John was governor).
August 1861	Joins the Confederate army in Cahaba.
September 9, 1861	Major in 20th Alabama Infantry.
October 8, 1861	Lieutenant colonel in 20th Alabama Infantry.
December 29, 1862	Captured at Stones River and later released in a prisoner exchange.
May 1, 1863	Captured at Port Gibson, Mississippi, but later escapes.
May 28, 1863	Colonel in 20th Alabama Infantry.
July 4, 1863	Captured at Vicksburg; exchanged on September 12, 1863.
September 18, 1863	Promoted to brigadier general.
November 25, 1863	Pettus and his brigade fight at Missionary Ridge.
June 27, 1864	Battle of Kennesaw Mountain.
July 22, 1864	Battle of Atlanta.
August 31– September 1, 1864	Battle of Jonesborough.

Date	Event(s)
March 19–21, 1865	Battle of Bentonville (North Carolina); Pettus is wounded in the leg.
May 2, 1865	Paroled in Salisbury, North Carolina.
October 20, 1865	Receives pardon from the Federal government.
1877	Grand dragon of the Alabama Ku Klux Klan.
March 4, 1897–July 27, 1907	U.S. senator from Alabama.
July 27, 1907	Dies in Hot Springs, North Carolina; buried at Live Oak Cemetery in Selma.
1940	Edmund Pettus Bridge is built in Selma to cross the Alabama River.
March 7, 1965	"Bloody Sunday" as civil rights marchers are attacked trying to cross the Edmund Pettus Bridge.
March 9, 1965	Martin Luther King Jr. decides not to cross the Edmund Pettus Bridge because of a federal injunction.
March 21, 1965	Selma to Montgomery March begins by crossing the Edmund Pettus Bridge.
March 11, 2013	Edmund Pettus Bridge is designated as a National Historic Landmark.
March 2015	On the fiftieth anniversary of Bloody Sunday, President Barack Obama, President George W. Bush and Georgia Representative John Lewis lead a march across the bridge. The *New York Times* carefully edits George Bush out of the group picture.

PHILLIP RODDEY

Brigadier General Phillip[19] Roddey was born about 1820[20] in Moulton, Alabama. At the time the war started, he was operating a steamboat on the

Tennessee River. Alarmed by the Union "Timberclad Raid" in February 1862 on northern Alabama, he destroyed his boat (so that it wouldn't fall into Union hands) and raised a mounted company that became part of the 4th Alabama Cavalry. On March 28, 1863, Roddey was placed in command of the Northern Alabama District, and on April 17, 1863, his forces helped push back the raid of Grenville Dodge into northwest Alabama. (The purpose of the raid was to provide a diversion to allow Colonel Abel Streight to infiltrate into northern Alabama.)

In the early part of the war, Roddey's company served as the escort of Braxton Bragg, including at the Battle of Shiloh. The following excerpt from *Alabama*, the seventh volume of the 1899 *Confederate Military History*, shows Bragg's high esteem for Roddey (emphasis added):

> *While Bragg was organizing for his Kentucky campaign, he advised General* [Sterling] *Price that* "Captain Roddey is detached with a squadron of cavalry on special service in northwest Alabama, where he has shown himself to be an officer of rare energy, enterprise and skill in harassing the enemy and procuring information of his movements. Captain Roddey has the entire confidence of the commanding general, who wishes to commend him to you as one eminently worthy of trust." *When it is remembered that the Federal forces were now in great strength at Corinth and vicinity, that Bragg proposed to move past them to the north, and Roddey was depended upon to watch the enemy, it will be seen that the captain was given an important trust. On August 21, 1862, General Bragg said in general orders:* "A portion of our cavalry, consisting of the companies of Earle, Lewis and Roddey, led by Captain Roddey, has made another brilliant dash upon a superior force of the enemy, resulting in their utter discomfiture and the capture of 123 prisoners. The judgment and prudence of the previous dispositions exhibit high military skill."[21]

On September 25, 1864 (after fighting in the Atlanta Campaign in Georgia), he was placed in charge of the north district of northern Alabama. Because of his close association with the northern part of Alabama, he is sometimes referred to as the "Defender of North Alabama."

General Roddey had a significant impact on Union brigadier general Edward M. McCook's retreat from Lovejoy Station, as part of McCook's raid during the Atlanta Campaign. McCook was supposed to join forces

"Philip Dale Roddey, 1826–1897." *Courtesy of the Library of Congress.*

with General Stoneman at Lovejoy Station, but Stoneman never showed, so McCook began to retreat back the way he had come—west, toward the Chattahoochee River.

Roddey and five hundred of his forces were stuck on railroad cars in Newnan, Georgia, because McCook had earlier destroyed the railroad infrastructure just north in Palmetto. On July 30, 1864, McCook's cavalry arrived in Newnan at 8:00 a.m. and had a bit of a surprise when they ran into Roddey's force. A brief skirmish ensued, and the Federals retreated, leaving McCook to find another route to get to the Chattahoochee River. This led directly to the Battle of Brown's Mill later in the day—perhaps Major General Joseph Wheeler's greatest moment as a general in the whole war.

After the Atlanta Campaign, Roddey served under Nathan Bedford Forrest in Alabama and helped defend the state against Wilson's Raid in March–April 1865. His last battle was the defense of Selma on April 2, 1865.

After the war, he lived in Tuscaloosa, Alabama, and then in New York City. He died during a business trip to London in 1897.

Date	Event(s)
circa 1820	Roddey is born in Moulton, Alabama.
November 6, 1845	Marries Margaret McGaughey (d. 1881).
1846	Appointed sheriff of Lawrence County.

Date	Event(s)
1860	Operates a steamboat on the Tennessee River.
April 1862	Raises a mounted company that becomes part of the 4th Alabama Cavalry and fights at the Battle of Shiloh.
December 1862	Commissioned colonel in 4th Alabama Cavalry.
March 28, 1863	Placed in command of the Northern Alabama District.
April 17, 1863	Pushes back the raid of Grenville Dodge in northwest Alabama; the purpose of the raid was to provide a diversion to allow Colonel Abel Streight to infiltrate into northern Alabama.
August 3, 1863	Promoted to brigadier general.
July 30, 1864	Helps disrupt McCook's Raid at Newnan, Georgia, during the Atlanta Campaign.
September 25, 1864	Placed in charge of the north district of northern Alabama.
April 1, 1865	Fights under Forrest at Ebenezer Church.
April 2, 1865	Participates in the defense of Selma against forces under Major General James Wilson.
May 1865	Surrenders to Union forces.
1866	Receives a Federal pardon.
July 20, 1897	Dies in London during a business trip and is buried at Greenwood Cemetery in Tuscaloosa.

ROBERT EMMETT RODES

Before the war, Robert Emmett[22] Rodes worked as an assistant professor at VMI, where he was beaten out by Thomas Jackson for a full professorship. After his teaching days, which ended in 1851, Rodes worked on a series of engineering jobs on various railroads, including the Southside Railroad in Virginia (home of the famous "High Bridge") and several railroads in Alabama.

Although born in Virginia, Rodes adopted Alabama as his homeland in 1857 when he married a Tuscaloosa girl, Virginia Hortense. When the war commenced in 1861, Rodes formed the 5th Alabama in Montgomery, Alabama, which elected Rodes as its colonel.

Rodes was soon promoted to brigadier general and fought in many engagements, including at Chancellorsville, Gettysburg, in the Overland Campaign and at the Wilderness, Spotsylvania and Cold Harbor. Rodes was killed at the Third Battle of Winchester by a shell fragment behind the ear.

Following is part of Rodes's report from July 1, 1863, at Gettysburg:

On July 1, in pursuance of the order to rejoin the army, the division resumed its march, but upon arriving at Middletown, and hearing that Lieutenant-General Hill's corps was moving upon Gettysburg, by order of General Ewell, the head of the column was turned in that direction: When within 4 miles of the town, to my surprise, the presence of the enemy there in force was announced by the sound of a sharp cannonade, and instant preparations for battle were made.

On arriving on the field, I found that by keeping along the wooded ridge, on the left side of which the town of Gettysburg is situated, I could strike the force of the enemy with which General Hill's troops were engaged upon the flank, and that, besides moving under cover, whenever we struck the enemy we could engage him with the advantage in ground.

The division was, therefore, moved along the summit of the ridge, with only one brigade deployed at first, and finally, as the enemy's cavalry had discovered us and the ground was of such character as to admit of cover for a large opposing force, with three brigades deployed; Doles on the left, Rodes' [old] brigade, Colonel O'Neal commanding, in the center, and Iverson on the right, the artillery and the other two brigades moved up closely to the line of battle. The division had to move nearly a mile before coming in view of the enemy's forces, excepting a few mounted men, and finally arrived at a point—a prominent hill on the ridge—whence the whole of that portion of the force opposing General Hill's troops could be seen. To get at these troops properly, which were still over half a mile from us, it was necessary to move the whole of my command by the right flank, and to change direction to the right.

While this was being done, Carter's battalion was ordered forward, and soon opened fire upon the enemy, who at this moment, as far as I could see, had no troops facing me at all. He had apparently been surprised; only a desultory fire of artillery was going on between his troops and General Hill's; but before my dispositions were made, the enemy began to show large bodies of men in front of the town, most of which were directed upon the position which I held, and almost at the same time a portion of the force opposed to General Hill changed position so as to occupy the woods on the summit of the same ridge I occupied (I refer to the forest touching the railroad and extending along the summit of the ridge toward my position as far as the Mummasburg road, which crossed the ridge at the base of the hill I held). Either these last troops, or others which had hitherto been unobserved behind the same body of woods, soon made their appearance directly opposite my center.

Being thus threatened from two directions, I determined to attack with my center and right, holding at bay still another force, then emerging from the town (apparently with the intention of turning my left), with Doles' brigade, which was moved somewhat to the left for this purpose, and trusting to this gallant brigade thus holding them until General Early's division arrived, which I knew would be soon, and which would strike this portion of the enemy's force on the flank before it could overpower Doles.

At this moment Doles' brigade occupied the open plain between the Middletown road and the foot of the ridge before spoken of. The Alabama brigade, with a wide interval between it and Doles', extended from this plain

"Rickett's advance against Rhodes [*sic*] division in the woods." *Courtesy of the Library of Congress.*

up the slope of the ridge; Daniel's brigade supported Iverson's, and extended some distance to the right of it; Ramseur was in reserve. All the troops were in the woods excepting Doles' and a portion of Rodes (O'Neal's) brigades, but all were subjected to some loss or annoyance from the enemy's artillery.

While making some examination into the position and apparent intentions of the enemy, with the view of attacking him, this artillery fire became so annoying that I ordered the Alabama brigade from the line it had occupied to fall back abreast with Iverson, so as to obtain some little shelter for the troops. The right regiment (Third Alabama) was, under my order, placed on a line with Daniel's brigade, Colonel O'Neal being instructed to form the balance of the brigade upon it. These dispositions were but temporary and unimportant, and are mentioned only because they are necessary to a full understanding of Colonel O'Neal's report.

Finding that the enemy was rash enough to come out from the woods to attack me, I determined to meet him when he got to the foot of the hill I occupied, and, as he did so, I caused Iverson's brigade to advance, and at the same moment gave in person to O'Neal the order to attack, indicating to him precisely the point to which he was to direct the left of the four regiments then under his orders, the Fifth Alabama, which formed the extreme left of this brigade, being held in reserve, under my own immediate command, to defend the gap between O'Neal and Doles. Daniel was at the same moment instructed to advance to support Iverson, if necessary; if not, to attack on his right as soon as possible.

Carter's whole battalion was by this time engaged hotly—a portion from the right, the remainder from the left of the hill—and was subjected to a heavy artillery fire in return. Iverson's brigade attacked handsomely, but suffered very heavily from the enemy's musketry fire from behind a stone wall along the crest of the ridge. The Alabama brigade went into action in some confusion, and with only three of its regiments (the Sixth, Twelfth, and Twenty-sixth), the Fifth having been retained by my order, and, for reasons explained to Colonel O'Neal, the Third having been permitted by Colonel O'Neal to move with Daniel's brigade.

The three first-mentioned regiments moved with alacrity (but not in accordance with my orders as to direction) and in confusion into the action. It was soon apparent that we were making no impression upon the enemy, and hence I ordered forward the Fifth Alabama to their support; but, to my surprise, in giving this command to its colonel (Hall). I found that Colonel O'Neal, instead of personally superintending the movements of his brigade, had chosen to remain with his reserve regiment. The result was that the whole brigade, with the exception of the Third Alabama (the movements of which will be seen by reference to the reports of Generals Ramseur and Iverson and Colonel Battle), was repulsed quickly, and with loss. Upon investigation recently, I find that just as O'Neal's men were about starting, and upon his informing me that he and his staff officers were not mounted, and that he had no mounted men with him, I permitted him to send Lieutenant [James] Arrington, of my staff, to Colonel Battle, commanding the Third Alabama Regiment, with his orders, and that Lieutenant Arrington delivered them to Colonel Battle.

Iverson's left being thus exposed; heavy loss was inflicted upon his brigade. His men fought and died like heroes. His dead lay in a distinctly marked line of battle. His left was overpowered, and many of his men, being surrounded, were captured.

General Daniel's gallant brigade, by a slight change in the direction of Iverson's attack, had been left too far to his right to assist him directly, and had already become engaged. The right of this brigade coming upon the enemy, strongly posted in a railroad cut, was, under its able commander's orders, thrown back skillfully, and the position of the whole brigade was altered so as to enable him to throw a portion of his force across the railroad, enfilade it, and attack to advantage.

After this change, General Daniel made a most desperate, gallant, and entirely successful charge upon the enemy, driving him at all points, but suffering terribly. The conduct of General Daniel and his brigade in this most desperate engagement elicited the admiration and praise of all who witnessed it. Just as his last effort was made, Ramseur's brigade, which under my orders had been so disposed as to support both Iverson and O'Neal, was ordered forward, and was hurled by its commander with the skill and gallantry for which he is always conspicuous, and with irresistible force, upon the enemy just where he had repulsed O'Neal and checked Iverson's advance.

In the meantime, General Early's division had been brought into action on my left with great success, and Doles, thus relieved, without waiting for orders, and though greatly outnumbered, boldly attacked the heavy masses of the enemy in his front. After a short but desperate contest, in which his brigade acted with unsurpassed gallantry, he succeeded in driving them before him, thus achieving on the left, and about the same time, a success no less brilliant than that of Ramseur, in the center, and Daniel, on the right.

In this affair, Doles handled his men with a skill and effect truly admirable, exhibiting marked coolness and courage.

O'Neal's shattered troops, which had assembled without order on the hill, rushed forward, still without order, but with all their usual courage, into the charge. Fry's battery, by my order, was pushed closely after Ramseur.

The Twelfth North Carolina, which had been held well in hand by Lieutenant-Colonel Davis, and the shattered remnants of the other regiments of Iverson's brigade, which had been rallied and organized by Capt. D.P. Halsey, assistant adjutant-general of the brigade, made under his guidance a dashing and effective charge just in time to be of considerable service to Ramseur and Daniel, and with them pressed closely after the enemy.

These successes were rapidly followed by a successful attack on my right on the part of General A.P. Hill's troops, who renewed their attack in time to put a stop to a murderous enfilade and reverse fire to which, in addition to the heavy direct fire it encountered, Daniel's brigade had been subjected from the time he commenced fairly his final advance.

The enemy was thus routed at all points. My division followed him closely into and through the town, Doles and Ramseur entering in such close contact with the enemy that the former, who penetrated the heart of the town first of all, had two sharp and successful encounters with the enemy in its streets, and the latter, who entered farther to the right, captured the colors of the One hundred and Fiftieth Pennsylvania Regiment in its streets, Lieutenant Harney, of his brigade, tearing them from the hands of the color-bearer, and falling almost immediately thereafter, mortally wounded.

In the pursuit, the division captured about 2,500 prisoners—so many as to embarrass its movements materially.[23]

At the Battle of Chancellorsville, he led a division during Jackson's flanking attack from the west.

Date	Event(s)
March 29, 1829	Rodes is born near Liberty, Bedford County, Virginia.
July 4, 1848	Graduates from Virginia Military Institute.
1848–51	Assistant professor at VMI.
1851–54	Assistant engineer for the Southside Railroad (Virginia).
1854–55	Works in railroad construction in Marshall, Tennessee.

April 1855	Briefly works on the Alabama Great Southern in Tuscaloosa, Alabama.
September 10, 1857	Marries Virginia Hortense in Tuscaloosa. They would have two children.
November 1857–61	Chief engineer of the Alabama and Chattanooga Railroad.
May 5, 1861	5th Alabama forms in Montgomery, Alabama, and elects Rodes as its colonel.
October 21, 1861	Promoted to brigadier general.
May 31, 1862	Leads a brigade at the Battle of Seven Pines, where he was severely wounded in the arm.
June 27, 1862	Leads a brigade at Haines's Mill but has to relinquish command because of his injuries at Seven Pines.
April 30–May 6, 1863	Leads a division at the Battle of Chancellorsville, including during Jackson's flanking attack from the west.
May 1863	Promoted to major general by Stonewall Jackson, while Jackson was on his deathbed.
July 1, 1863	Leads the assault against the right flank of the Union I Corps at Gettysburg.
1864	Fights under Richard Ewell during the Overland Campaign of Ulysses S. Grant. Fights under Jubal Early in the Valley Campaigns of 1864.
September 19, 1864	Killed at the Third Battle of Winchester by a shell fragment behind the ear.

EMMA SANSOM

Emma Sansom was born in Social Circle, Georgia, in 1847, but her family migrated to Gadsden, Alabama, around 1852. It was here where Emma would stake her claim as the greatest heroine of Alabama during the Civil War.

On May 2, 1863, Nathan Bedford Forrest was pursuing forces led by Colonel Abel Straight in the Gadsden area. After forces under Streight burned the only bridge over Black Creek (which runs north–south through modern-day Gadsden), Forrest was looking for someone who could show him an alternate path across Black Creek. The someone turned out to be sixteen-year-old Emma Sansom, who rode behind Forrest to show him where he could ford the creek.

As a result of her efforts, Streight was captured the next day (May 3, 1863) at the Battle of Cedar Bluff, Alabama. The Alabama legislature awarded Emma a gold medal in 1864 and a plot of land in 1899 for her heroism.

Following are two sources that describe her efforts (the second is from Emma Sansom herself):

As they looked down the road they saw one single blue-uniformed man riding at highest speed, rushing along the highway as if mad, waving his hands and beating his tired mount with his sword. Just behind him, at full speed, came other men, shooting at the fleeing Federals. In front of the humble [Sansom] home the single horseman suddenly stopped and threw up his hands and cried "I surrender. I surrender." Then up to his side rode with rapid stride a soldier in gray. He had some stars on his collar and a wreath about them, and he said to the women, "I am a Confederate general. I am trying to capture and kill the Yankee soldiers across the creek yonder."

Standing on the front porch of the house, these women watched these startling and surprising proceedings. The leader who was pursuing this single soldier in blue sat on his panting steed at the gate. The young girls knew that the gray uniform meant friends, rescue, kindness, chivalry. They walked to the fence and outside the gate touched the bridle of their deliverer's steed and patted his foam-covered neck and looked up into the face of the stern soldier, without fear or dread.

With tones as tender as those of a woman, the officer who had captured the Federal vidette [mounted sentry] said, "Do not be alarmed. I am General Forrest, and I will protect you." Other men in gray came riding in great haste and speedily dismounting left their horses and scattered out into the forest on either side of the road. The youngest girl told the Confederate general that the Yankees were amongst the trees on the other side of the creek, and they would kill him if he went down toward the bridge. She did not realize how little the man in gray feared the shooting. Now the flames from the burning rails and bridge timbers began to hiss and the crackling wood told that the bridge was going into smoke and ashes and no human power could save it from ruin.

The leader said, "I must get across. I must catch these raiders. Can we ford the creek, or are there any other bridges near?" "There is no bridge you can cross," the younger girl replied, "but you and your men can get across down there in the woods. If you will saddle me a horse, I'll go and show you where it is; I have seen the cows wade there and I am sure you, too, can cross it." "Little girl," the general exclaimed, "there's no time for saddling horses. Get up behind me," and seeing a low bank, he pointed her there. She sprang with the agility of an athlete upon the bank, and then with a quick leap seated herself behind the grim horseman, catching onto his waist with her hands. The soldier pushed his spurs into the flanks of the doubly burdened horse and started in a gallop through the woods, by the father's grave, along the path indicated by his youthful guide.

The mother cried out in alarm, and with ill-concealed fear bade her child dismount. General Forrest quietly said, "Don't be alarmed; I'll take good care of her and bring her safely back. She's only going to show me the ford where I can cross the creek and catch the Yankees over yonder before they can get to Rome." There was something in the look of the warrior that stilled fear for her child, and with eager gaze, half-way consenting, she watched them as they galloped across the corn field. They were soon lost to sight in the timbered ravine through which the soldier man and the maiden so firmly seated behind him now passed out of view. Following the branch a short distance, General Forrest found that it entered Black Creek three-fourths of a mile above the bridge. Through the trees and underbrush, as she saw the muddy waters of the stream, she warned her companion that they were where they could be seen by the enemy, and they had better get down from the horse. Without waiting for the assistance of her escort, she unloosed her hold and sprang to the earth.[24]

Emma Sansom told the rest of the story in her own words:

We rode out into a field through which ran a small ravine and along which there was a thick undergrowth that protected us for a while from being seen by the Yankees at the bridge and on the other side of the creek. This branch emptied into the creek just above the ford. When we got close to the creek, I said: "General Forrest, I think we had better get off the horse, as we are now where we may be seen." We both got down and crept through the bushes, and when we were right at the ford I happened to be in front. He stepped quickly between me and the Yankees, saying: "I am glad to have you for a pilot, but I am not going to make breastworks of you." The cannon and the other guns were firing fast by this time, as I pointed out to him where to go into the water and out on the other bank, and then went back towards the house. He asked me my name, and asked me to give him a lock of my hair. The cannon-balls were screaming over us so loud we were told to leave and hide in some place out of danger, which we did. Soon all the firing stopped, and I started back home. On the way I met General Forrest again, and he told me that he had written a note for me and left it on the bureau. He asked me again for a lock of my hair, and as we went into the house he said: "One of my bravest men has been killed, and he is laid out in the house. His name is Robert Turner. I want you to see that he is buried in some graveyard near here." He then told me good-bye and got on his horse, and he and his men rode away and left us all alone. My sister and I sat up all night watching over the dead soldier, who had lost his life fighting for our rights, in which we were overpowered, but never conquered. General Forrest and his men endeared themselves to us forever.[25]

Date	Event(s)
June 2, 1847	Sansom is born in Social Circle, Georgia.
circa 1852	Family moves to Gadsden, Alabama.
May 2, 1863	Sixteen-year-old Emma Sansom rides behind Nathan Bedford Forrest to show him where he could ford Black Creek in the ongoing battle between Forrest and troops under Abel Streight (Streight had burned the only bridge across Black Creek shortly before).
May 3, 1863	Battle of Cedar Bluff, Alabama, in which Abel Streight is captured by Nathan Bedford Forrest. Streight will be sent to Libby Prison.
1864	Alabama legislature votes Emma Sansom a gold medal and a plot of land.
October 29, 1864	Marries Christopher B. Johnson.
circa 1868 (or 1876)	Moves to Texas.

Date	Event(s)
1887	Husband Christopher dies, leaving her to care for five girls and two boys.
1899	Alabama legislature votes her a second plot of land.
August 9, 1900	Dies in Upshur County, Texas.
1907	Monument erected on the west side of the Broad Street Bridge in Gadsden, Alabama.
1911	John Trotwood Moore writes "A Ballad of Emma Sansom."
1929	Emma Sansom High School is built in what is now Gadsden, Alabama.
2006	Emma Sansom High School becomes Emma Sansom Middle School.

RAPHAEL SEMMES

Rear Admiral Raphael Semmes is perhaps the most famous of all Confederate naval officers. He was in command of two of the most famous commerce raiders of the war: the CSS *Sumter* and the CSS *Alabama*. Between those two ships, more than eighty Union commerce vessels were captured or destroyed. While some people referred to the *Alabama* as a "privateer" or "pirate," Semmes rejected that classification:

> The Alabama *having been built by the Government of the Confederate States, and commissioned by these States, as a ship of war, was, in no sense of the word, a* privateer, *which is a private armed ship belonging to individuals, and fitted out for purposes of gain. And yet, throughout the whole war, and long after the war, when she was not called a "pirate" by the Northern press, she was called a* privateer. *Even high Government officials of the enemy so characterized her. Many of the newspapers erred through ignorance, but this misnomer was sheer malice, and very petty malice, too, on the part of those of them who were better informed, and on the part of the Government officials, all of whom, of course, knew better. Long after they had acknowledged the war, as a war, which carried with it an acknowledgment of the right of the*

Confederate States to fit out cruisers, they stultified themselves by calling her "pirate," and "privateer." They were afraid to speak the truth, in conformity with the facts, lest the destruction of their property, for which they hoped ultimately to be paid, should seem to be admitted to have been done under the sanction of the laws of nations. They could as logically have called General Robert E. Lee a bandit, *as myself a* pirate; *but logic was not the* forte *of the enemy, either during or since the late war.*[26]

Semmes also has the distinction of being the only officer in the war to be promoted to both rear admiral and brigadier general. This strange series of events was kicked off after

Left: Raphael Semmes. *Courtesy of the Library of Congress.*

Below: "Duncan Place and Semmes Monument, Mobile, Ala.," circa 1900. *Courtesy of the Library of Congress.*

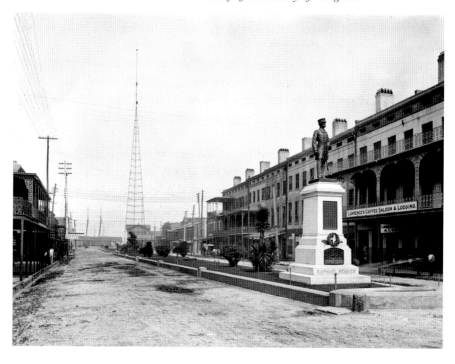

the fall of Richmond, when Semmes ordered the ships of the James River Squadron destroyed so as to not fall into Union hands. After their destruction, Semmes's sailors became soldiers, known as the "Naval Brigade," and fought on land.

The Naval Brigade surrendered to William Tecumseh Sherman at Durham, North Carolina, on April 1862. Semmes discussed his receiving of the army rank in his memoirs:

> *I found, at Danville, President Davis, and a portion of his cabinet—the Secretary of the Navy among the rest. Here was temporarily established the seat of Government. I called on the President and Secretary, who were staying at the same house, at an early hour on the morning after my arrival, and reported for duty. They were both calm in the presence of the great disaster which had befallen them and the country. Mr. Mallory could scarcely be said now to have a portfolio, though he still had the officers and clerks of his Department around him. It was at once arranged between him, and the President, that my command should be organized as a brigade of artillery, and assigned to the defences around Danville. The question of my rank being discussed, it was settled by Mr. Davis, that I should act in the capacity of a brigadier-general. My grade being that of a rear-admiral, I was entitled to rank, relatively, with the officers of the army, as a major-general, but it was folly, of course, to talk of rank, in the circumstances in which we were placed, and so I contented myself by saying pleasantly to the President, that I would waive the matter of rank, to be discussed hereafter, if there should ever be occasion to discuss it. "That is the right spirit," said he, with a smile playing over his usually grave features. I did not see him afterward. He moved soon to Charlotte, in North Carolina, and in a few weeks afterward, he fell into the hands of the enemy.*[27]

Semmes's *Memoirs of Service Afloat: During the War Between the States* is one of the most vivid firsthand accounts of the Civil War.

Date	Event(s)
September 27, 1809	Semmes is born in Charles County, Maryland.
1826	Graduates from Charlotte Hall Military Academy.
	Enters the U.S. Navy as a midshipman.

Date	Event(s)
1846	During the Mexican-American War, Semmes commands the USS *Somers*, which is lost in a storm near Veracruz in December 1846.
post–Mexican War	Practices law in Mobile, Alabama; writes *Service Afloat and Ashore During the Mexican War*.
1855	Promoted to commander.
January 1861	Resigns from the U.S. Navy.
April 1861	Becomes the commander of the commerce raider CSS *Sumter* in New Orleans; the *Sumter* would go on to destroy eighteen Union ships.
August 1862–June 1864	Captain of the CSS *Alabama*, the most successful Confederate raider of the war (sixty-five Union ships captured or destroyed).
June 19, 1864	The *Alabama* is destroyed off the port of Cherbourg by the USS *Kearsarge*; Semmes escapes to England on the British yacht *Deerhound*.
February 1865	Promoted to rear admiral and given command of the James River Squadron.
April 1865	After the fall of Richmond, Semmes destroys his squadron's ships and is appointed a brigadier general in the Confederate States Army; his sailors become the Naval Brigade and fight on land—most of them, including Semmes, go to fight with Joe Johnston's army in North Carolina.
April 26, 1865	Semmes's forces surrender to William Tecumseh Sherman and are paroled.
December 15, 1865	Arrested for treason and incarcerated.
April 7, 1866	Released from prison and becomes a teacher at what is now LSU.
1869	Writes *Memoirs of Service Afloat During the War Between the States*.

Date	Event(s)
1871	Presented with a house by the citizens of Mobile.
August 30, 1877	Dies in Mobile, Alabama, from food poisoning.
November 1900	Semmes Land Company Inc. is founded and begins plotting out Semmes, Alabama.

JOHN GILL SHORTER

John Gill Shorter was born in Monticello, Georgia, in 1818. He moved with his family to Alabama (near modern-day Eufaula) in 1833.

Prior to the war, he served as a lawyer; a state senator from Barbour County, Alabama (1845); in the statehouse (1851); and as an elected circuit judge (1852). In 1861, he was appointed to the secession committee in Georgia by Alabama governor Andrew B. Moore.

In August of the same year, he was elected to governor of Alabama on a promise of limited government. Like other Southern governors of the time, he was immediately presented with a dilemma. He had campaigned on a platform of states' rights and limited government, but as soon as he was elected, the Confederate government started making demands of him that impinged on state sovereignty. For example, in 1862, he supported conscription as imposed by the Confederate government and supported a law that required slaveholders to provide slaves for building defenses in the state of Alabama. Neither action was popular with staunchly independent Alabamians. He lost his reelection bid in 1863 to Thomas Hill Watts.

After the war, he went back to being a lawyer in Eufaula, Alabama. He died there in 1872.

Date	Event(s)
April 3, 1818	Shorter is born in Monticello, Georgia.
1833	Family moves to what is modern-day Eufaula, Alabama.
1837	Graduates from the University of Georgia and establishes a law practice in Alabama.
1843	Marries Mary Jane Battle in Eufaula, Alabama.

"Governor Shorter House, Montgomery, Alabama." *Courtesy of the Library of Congress.*

Date	Event(s)
1845	Becomes state senator from Barbour County, Alabama.
1851	Gains statehouse seat.
1852	Elected circuit judge.
1861	Appointed to secession committee in Georgia by Alabama governor Andrew B. Moore. Elected to governor of Alabama on a promise of limited government (August).
April 1862	Supports conscription imposed by the Confederate government.
October 1862	Supports an enacted law requiring slaveholders to provide slaves for building defenses in the state of Alabama.

Date	Event(s)
1863	After initial opposition, Shorter supports a bill requiring the state to provide food to the indigent. Loses gubernatorial election to Thomas Hill Watts.
post–Civil War	Returns to practicing law in Eufaula, Alabama.
May 29, 1872	Dies in Eufaula, Alabama.

THOMAS HILL WATTS

Thomas Watts was born in 1819 in Butler County, Alabama. Prior to the war, he practiced law and served in the state House of Representatives. He was also a plantation owner, owning 179 slaves.

As the war began, he served as a representative to the Alabama Secession Convention. In August 1861, he formed and became colonel of the 17th Regiment Alabama Infantry. In the same year, he ran for governor in Georgia and lost to John Gill Shorter.

Thomas Hill Watts.

In 1862, he was appointed attorney general of the Confederacy by Jefferson Davis and assisted in creating the Supreme Court of the Confederacy. He upheld the constitutionality of the Conscription Act of 1862.

In 1863, he ran again for governor of Alabama, and this time he beat John Gill Shorter in the gubernatorial election. As governor, he faced an insurmountable list of problems, including rampant inflation, the unpopularity of conscription, an inefficient state militia system and a faction in the state government that advocated peace talks with the Union. His eighteen-month reign as governor ended on May 1, 1865, when he was briefly arrested by Union troops near Union Springs, Alabama. He decided not to try to run for reelection after the war ended.

After the war, he practiced law in Montgomery, Alabama, where he died on September 16, 1892.

Date	Event(s)
January 3, 1819	Watts is born in Butler County, Alabama.
1840	Graduates from University of Virginia with a law degree. Begins practicing law in Greenville, Butler County.
1842–45	Serves in the state House of Representatives.
1846	Begins practicing law in Montgomery.
1855	Runs for the U.S. House of Representatives as a Know-Nothing and loses.
1860	As a plantation owner, he owns 179 slaves.
January 4, 1861	State militia seizes Forts Morgan and Gaines.
January 7, 1861	Representative to the Alabama Secession Convention. Secession passes sixty-one to thirty-nine.
August 1861	Forms and becomes colonel of the 17th Regiment Alabama Infantry.
1861	Loses election for governor to John Gill Shorter.
1862	Appointed attorney general of the Confederacy by Jefferson Davis and assists in creating the Supreme Court of the Confederacy. Upholds constitutionality of the Conscription Act of 1862.

Date	Event(s)
December 1, 1863	Becomes governor of Alabama (beating John Gill Shorter in the gubernatorial election).
May 1, 1865	Briefly arrested by Union troops near Union Springs, Alabama.
post–Civil War	Practices law in Montgomery, Alabama.
September 16, 1892	Dies in Montgomery, Alabama.

MAJOR GENERAL JOSEPH WHEELER

Joseph Wheeler was, along with Nathan Bedford Forrest, the most significant Confederate cavalry officer in the west during the Civil War. Wheeler fought in a number of battles and raids throughout the war, including at Shiloh and in the Chickamauga Campaign, the Tullahoma Campaign, the Chattanooga Campaign, the Knoxville Campaign, the Carolinas Campaign and Sherman's Atlanta Campaign and March to the Sea. He was a key player in the defeat of the Stoneman/McCook Raid into central Georgia in July 1864.

Wheeler's was the sole Confederate (as opposed to militia) fighting force that challenged Sherman during the March to the Sea. Most of his battles with Sherman were with his opposing number, Judson Kilpatrick, but a few times he had Union infantry arrayed against him (Griswoldville and Waynesboro). He successfully helped defend Macon against a cavalry raid by Kilpatrick in the early days of the March.

There was some controversy regarding Wheeler's performance during the war. He was criticized for not letting Braxton Bragg know the location of Rosecrans's army in the month leading up to the Battle of Chickamauga. He was relieved of his position as head of the cavalry for the Army of Tennessee during Sherman's Carolinas Campaign because of a review by a staff officer named Colonel Roman.

Beauregard's staff had criticized the lax discipline in Wheeler's corps. Interestingly, the officers of "Camp Humes's Cavalry Division, In The Field, Wayne County, N. C., April 3d, 1865," wrote a document in strong support of their longtime leader, Joseph Wheeler:

Right: Major General Joseph Wheeler, 1836–1906. *Courtesy of the Library of Congress.*

Below: "General Joseph Wheeler House, State Highway 20, Wheeler, Lawrence County, AL." *Courtesy of the Library of Congress.*

Resolved 1st, That since the organization of this cavalry corps we have followed General Wheeler, and have always found him vigilant, active and brave, and that during this long period, now over eighteen months, he has never been absent from his post for an hour, constantly giving his personal attention to the interests of the cause. He has been foremost in fight, in most instances even leading and directing the movements of the skirmish line. In every exigency his presence inspiring the utmost confidence on the part of all his troops…

…Resolved 4th, That, while we would not underrate the distinguished services rendered or detract from the merited laurels won by General Hampton, we desire to say in most unmistakable terms that we entertain now, as we have always done, the most unbounded confidence in General Wheeler as a man and as an officer, and where he leads we will cheerfully follow.[28]

Wheeler served as a major general of volunteers in the Spanish-American War and had Theodore Roosevelt's Rough Riders under his command.

Date	Event(s)
September 10, 1836	Wheeler is born in Augusta, Georgia.
July 1, 1859	Graduates from West Point, nineteenth out of twenty-two in his class.
June 26, 1860	Serves in the Regiment of Mounted Rifles in the New Mexico Territory.
September 1, 1860	Promoted to the rank of second lieutenant.
March 16, 1861	Joins the Confederate army as a first lieutenant, serving in the Georgia state militia artillery.
September 4, 1861	Promoted to colonel of the 19th Alabama Infantry Regiment.
April 1862	Serves under Braxton Bragg at the Battle of Shiloh.
September–October 1862	Given command of the 2nd Cavalry Brigade of the Left Wing in the Army of Mississippi.

Date	Event(s)
October 30, 1862	Promoted to brigadier general after fighting at Perryville.
November 27, 1862	Injured at La Vergne, Tennessee, from an artillery shell.
December 1862	Successful cavalry raid against the Army of the Cumberland during its advance from Nashville.
1863	Writes *A Revised System of Cavalry Tactics, for the Use of the Cavalry and Mounted Infantry, C.S.A.*
January 12–13, 1863	Effective cavalry raid against Union forces in Tennessee at Harpeth Shoals.
January 20, 1863	Upon Bragg's recommendation, promoted to major general.
May 1, 1863	Receives "Thanks of the Confederate Congress" for his action at Harpeth Shoals.
September 1863	Criticized for not letting Braxton Bragg know the location of Rosecrans's army in the month leading up to the Battle of Chickamauga.
September 19–20, 1863	Cavalry commander at the Battle of Chickamauga.
October 2, 1863	Successful cavalry raid at Anderson's Cross Roads in central Tennessee.
November 25–27, 1863	Covers Bragg's retreat into north Georgia after the Battle of Missionary Ridge.
July 30, 1864	Routs Edward McCook's cavalry at the Battle of Brown's Mill.
August 14–15, 1864	Cavalry raid on Dalton, Georgia—tears up some W&A track, but the Union garrison there doesn't surrender.
Late August 1864	Raiding in Tennessee, Wheeler's cavalry is not present during the final days of Hood's defense of Atlanta.

ALABAMA AND THE CIVIL WAR

Date	Event(s)
November–December 1864	Wheeler is the only effective fighting force against Sherman during the latter's March to the Sea.
February 11, 1865	Defeats Union brigadier general Judson Kilpatrick at Aiken, South Carolina, but is soon relieved of his command of the Confederate cavalry and placed under the command of Wade Hampton.
March 19–20, 1865	Fights under Hampton at the Battle of Bentonville, North Carolina.
May 1865	Wheeler is captured by Union troops in Conyer's Station, Georgia, and imprisoned at Fort Monroe.
June 8, 1865	Wheeler is paroled and released from confinement.
1882	Wins special election to the U.S. Congress.
1883	Authors *Fitz-John Porter*.
1884–1900	Becomes U.S. congressman.
1898	Appointed major general of volunteers by President William McKinley to head cavalry forces in Cuba. Appears in silent film *Surrender of General Toral* (with William Rufus Shafter).
June 24, 1898	Battle of Las Guasimas, Cuba (near Santiago).
July 1, 1898	Battle of San Juan Hill. Theodore Roosevelt and the Rough Riders serve under Wheeler.
1899	Authors *Confederate Military History: Alabama*. Authors *The Santiago Campaign*.
August 1899	Commands 1st Brigade, 2nd Division in the Philippine-American War.
June 16, 1900	Commissioned as brigadier general in the regular army.

Date	Event(s)
January 25, 1906	Dies in New York City and is buried at Arlington Cemetery.
November 5, 1912	Wheeler County, Georgia, is established (located southeast of Macon).
July 18, 1917	Camp Wheeler, Macon, is established (decommissioned on January 19, 1946).
1936	Wheeler Lake and Wheeler Dam in Alabama are opened.
1938	Wheeler National Wildlife Refuge near Decatur, Alabama, is opened.
1965	Joseph Wheeler High School in Marietta, Georgia, is opened.
1997	Portrayed by Gary Busey in the miniseries *Rough Riders*.

MAJOR GENERAL JAMES H. WILSON

James H. Wilson, who graduated from West Point Military Academy in 1860 as a brevet second lieutenant, rose to the rank of major general by the end of the war. His greatest fame would come in March–April 1865, when he launched Wilson's Raid across Alabama and Georgia. During this time, he captured Montgomery and Selma, Alabama, as well as Columbus, West Point and Macon, Georgia. Along the way,

"Portrait of Maj. Gen. (as of May 6, 1865) James H. Wilson, officer of the Federal Army." *Courtesy of the Library of Congress.*

he destroyed a number of Confederate ironworks, machine shops and naval facilities (including burning the unfinished ironclad ram CSS *Jackson* in Columbus, Georgia).

For good measure, his troops would capture Jefferson Davis near Irwinville, Georgia, on May 10, 1865, and also capture Major General Howell Cobb in Macon on April 20, 1865. Wilson ordered the arrest of Andersonville commandant Henry Wirz on May 7, 1865. The following excerpt from a Northern newspaper gives some sense of Wilson's impact during the famous raid:

WILSON'S CAMPAIGN.

At any other period of the war, the terrible blows dealt the enemy by our Western cavalry in this adventurous campaign would have thrilled the country with a sense of triumph. This expedition by Wilson is the great "raid" of the war. An examination of a map is necessary to understanding fully the daring and destructive sweep made through the very heart of the Gulf States. In the first place the famous rebel cavalry, under Forrest, was defeated and almost annihilated at Selma, Alabama, and the rebel arsenals and manufactories at that place destroyed. The main body of our forces moved eastward, capturing Montgomery, West Point, Columbus and Macon, making apparently for Savannah, scattering the militia on all sides, ruining the only remaining strand of railroad that might be of use to the rebels, breaking up their machine shops, and annihilating not only their military stores but rendering the manufacture of material for future campaigns impossible. We do not wonder that Joe Johnston said to General Sherman, of Wilson, "Stop him, for God's sake, for he is raiding through the country and tearing everything to pieces."[29]

Wilson is sometimes compared favorably to William Tecumseh Sherman, as Wilson's Raid was very destructive of Confederate factories, armories and naval installations but had much less impact on civilians than Sherman's Atlanta Campaign, March to the Sea or Carolinas Campaign.

Date	Event(s)
September 2, 1837	Wilson is born in Shawneetown, Illinois.
1860	Graduates from West Point, sixth in his class, as a brevet second lieutenant.

Date	Event(s)
September 1861–March 1862	Topographical engineer for the Port Royal Expeditionary Force.
April 10–11, 1862	Topographical engineer for the Department of the South, at the Battle of Fort Pulaski; promoted to major.
April 1862	Topographic engineer for the Army of the Potomac and aide-de-camp to Major General George McClellan during the Maryland Campaign.
late 1862–early 1863	Inspector general for Grant's army during the Vicksburg Campaign.
October 30, 1863	Promoted to brigadier general of volunteers; participates in the Chattanooga Campaign.
February 17, 1864	Chief of the Cavalry Bureau in Washington, D.C.
May 6, 1864	Promoted to brevet major general by Grant and assigned to duty under Philip Sheridan; Wilson commands a cavalry division during the Overland and Valley Campaigns.
June 22, 1864	Begins a cavalry raid near Petersburg. He tears up sixty miles of track but is defeated near a bridge over the Staunton River.
October 1864	Brevet major general of volunteers; Wilson is transferred back to the west and becomes chief of cavalry for the Military Division of the Mississippi (now under Sherman).
November–December 1864	Attached to George Thomas's army and fights at Franklin and Nashville; he will be promoted to brevet brigadier general in the regular army for his service at the latter.
November 30, 1864	Beats back Forrest at the Battle of Franklin.
March–April 1865	Wilson's Raid commences through Alabama and Georgia. He captures Montgomery, Selma, Columbus, West Point and Macon.
March 31, 1865	Destroys Shelby Iron Works, Roupes Valley Ironworks at Tannehill and Bibb Naval Furnace at Brierfield.

Date	Event(s)
April 2, 1865	Battle of Selma—Forrest defeated.
April 4, 1865	Burns the University of Alabama at Tuscaloosa (a military school).
April 12, 1865	Occupies Montgomery.
April 16, 1865	Battle of West Point—the Union takes Fort Tyler. Battle of Columbus—Wilson's forces take the city and destroy the Confederate ram CSS *Jackson*.

Later By Telegraph!!

WILSON ROUTS FORREST AT EBENEZER CHURCH!!

Selma, Montgomery, Columbus, West Point and Macon Taken!

GENS. HOWELL COBB, GUSTAVUS SMITH, ROBISON, MERCER AND McCALL, 1,500 PRISONERS, 48 GUNS, AND 100,000 BALES OF COTTON CAP-TURED!!!

Jeff. and the Leading Conspirators to be Indicted!!

A DEMAND TO BE MADE ON CANADA FOR THE SURRENDER OF THE CON-SPIRATORS THERE!!

JEFF. AND HIS CANADIAN COMMIS-SIONERS PROVED GUILTY OF THE CONSPIRACY!!

Great Flood on the Mississippi!!!

The Forts About Washington to be Dismantled!!

New York, 4.

"Selma, Montgomery, Columbus, West Point and Macon Taken!" *From the* Montana Post, *May 20, 1865.*

Date	Event(s)
April 20, 1865	Macon surrenders, and Major General Howell Cobb is captured.
May 5, 1865	Henry Wirz, commandant of Andersonville, is arrested.
May 10, 1865	Jefferson Davis is arrested outside Irwinville, Georgia.
February 23, 1925	Dies in Wilmington, Delaware.

WILLIAM LOWNDES YANCEY

William Lowndes Yancey was a Southern plantation owner, newspaper editor and politician who spoke out strongly in favor of states' rights, secession and preserving the Southern way of life in the 1850s. He also stressed the need for constitutional protection of minorities (similar to the views of John C. Calhoun). He was known for his oratorical skills and was perhaps the greatest orator in the South in the years leading up to the war. He also served as the head of the Confederate States of America Diplomatic Mission to Europe in 1861–62.

Yancey is probably the person most responsible for splitting the Democratic party into Northern and Southern factions in 1860, a move that ultimately led to the election of Republican Abraham Lincoln the same year. Following is an excerpt from his speech at the 1860 Democratic Convention:

The South is in a minority, we have been tauntingly told to-day. In the progress of events and the march of civilization and emigration, the Northwest has grown up, from a mere infant in swaddling clothes, at the formation of the Constitution, into the form and proportions of a giant people; and owing to its institutions and demand for white labor, and the peculiar nature of our institutions, tho advancing side by side with us in parallel lines, but never necessarily in conflict, it has surpassed us greatly in numbers. We are, therefore, in a numerical minority. But we do not murmur at this; we cheerfully accept the result; but we as firmly claim the right of the minority—and what is that? We claim the benefit of the Constitution that was made for the protection of minorities.

In the march of events, feeling conscious of your numerical power, you have aggressed upon us. We hold up between us and your advancing columns of numbers that written instrument which your and our fathers made, and by the compact of which, you with your power were to respect as to us and our rights. Our and your fathers made it that they and their children should for ever observe it; that, upon all questions affecting the rights of the minority, the majority should not rely upon their voting numbers, but should look, in restraint upon passion, avarice and lust for power, to the written compact, to see in what the minority was to be respected, and how it was to be protected, and to yield an implicit obedience to that compact. Constitutions are made solely for the protection of the minorities in government, and for the guidance of majorities.

Ours are now the institutions which are at stake; ours is the peace that is to be destroyed; ours is the property that is to be destroyed; ours is the honor at stake—the honor of children, the honor of families, the lives, perhaps, of all of us. It all rests upon what your course may ultimately make out of a great heaving volcano of passion. Bear with us then, while we stand sternly upon what is yet a dormant volcano, and say that we can yield no position until we are convinced that we are wrong. We are in a position to ask you to yield. What right of yours, gentlemen of the North, have we of the South ever invaded? What institution of yours have we ever assailed, directly or indirectly? What laws have we ever passed that have invaded, or induced others to invade, the sanctity of your homes, or to put your lives in jeopardy, or that were likely to destroy the fundamental institutions of your States? The wisest, the most learned and the best among you remain silent, because you can not say that we have done this thing.[30]

Date	Event(s)
August 10, 1814	Yancey is born in Warren County, Georgia.
1833	Leaves Williams College in Massachusetts six weeks before graduation.
July 4, 1834	Gives a speech in Greenville, South Carolina, against secession.
August 13, 1834	Marries Sarah Caroline Earl.
November 1834	Becomes editor of the *Greenville Mountaineer.*

Date	Event(s)
winter 1836–37	Moves to his wife's plantation near Cahaba, Alabama.
1838	Becomes editor of the *Cahaba Southern Democrat*; writes an editorial in defense of slavery.
September 1838	In an "affair of honor," Yancey kills a man in Greenville, South Carolina, and serves several months in jail for manslaughter.
1841	Elected to Alabama House of Representatives.
1843	Elected to Alabama Senate.
December 2, 1844–September 1, 1846	Becomes U.S. congressman from Alabama.
1850s	Member of the "Fire-Eaters,"[31] a group of Southern politicians in favor of forming a new nation out of the Southern states.
February 1851	Gives "Address to the People of Alabama," which criticizes northern treatment of the South.
spring 1860	At the Democratic National Convention, he advocates splitting the Democratic Party into Northern and Southern factions; Southern delegates nominate John C. Breckinridge for president.
October 10, 1860	Speech at Cooper Institute Hall in New York warning Northerners of dire consequences if attempts are made to abolish slavery.
January 1861	Alabama secedes, with Yancey leading the way; Jefferson Davis is sworn in as president in Montgomery, Alabama, and Yancey makes a speech of welcome ("The man and the hour have met").
February 18, 1861	Turns down a cabinet position but agrees to a diplomatic post.

Date	Event(s)
March 16, 1861–January 29, 1862	Head of Confederate States of America Diplomatic Mission to Europe.
May 12, 1861	Queen Victoria announces a policy of neutrality regarding the American conflict.
February 18, 1862–July 27, 1863	Becomes Confederate States senator from Alabama.
July 27, 1863	Dies in Montgomery, Alabama, of kidney disease.

Chapter 2

Alabama Civil War Timeline

The Civil War in Alabama began in January 4, 1861, when Alabama militia seized Forts Gaines and Morgan, as well as the Mount Vernon Arsenal. (Note that all three events occurred before Alabama seceded from the Union.)

The Civil War in Alabama ended officially on May 8, 1865, when forces under General Richard Taylor surrendered in Citronelle, Alabama, to Major General Edward Canby. Nathan Bedford Forrest surrendered the next day in Gainesville, Alabama. The war was over.

Date	Event(s)
January 4, 1861	Alabama militia seize Fort Morgan and Fort Gaines in Mobile Bay. Alabama militia seize the Mount Vernon Arsenal (north of Mobile).
January 11, 1861	Alabama secedes by a vote of sixty-one to thirty-nine.
February 9, 1861	Constitutional Convention in Montgomery, Alabama, considers Jefferson Davis, Robert Toombs, Howell Cobb and Alexander Stephens for the presidency.
February 18, 1861	Davis is inaugurated as provisional president of the Confederacy in Montgomery, Alabama.

Date	Event(s)
May 1861	Confederate capital moves to Richmond, Virginia
February 6, 1862	Three Union gunboats reach Florence, Alabama (northwest Alabama), on the Tennessee River.
April 11, 1862	Huntsville is occupied by Union forces under Ormsby Mitchel.
May 1862	The city of Athens is burned and looted by Union troops.
April 1863	Colonel Abel Streight begins a Union raid into northern Alabama via Tuscumbia.
May 3, 1863	Battle of Cedar Bluff, Alabama, in which Abel Streight is captured by Nathan Bedford Forrest. Streight will be sent to Libby Prison.
July 1863	Submarine *H.L. Hunley* is launched in Mobile, after being built at the Park and Lyons Machine shop in the city.
winter 1863–64	Union general John Logan and the 15th Army Corps spend the winter in Huntsville.
April 12–16, 1864	Raid of Union brigadier general John W. Geary down the Tennessee River from Bridgeport to Triana.
July 1864	General Rousseau leads a raid down the Coosa River and destroys railroad infrastructure in Auburn, Opelika and Loachapoka, Alabama.
July 14, 1864	Forces under Union major general Lovell H. Rousseau destroy Janney Furnace.
August 5, 1864	Federal victory under Admiral David Farragut at the Battle of Mobile Bay. "Damn the torpedoes. Full speed ahead!"
August 8, 1864	Fort Gaines is surrendered by Colonel Charles D. Anderson.
August 23, 1864	Brigadier General Richard L. Page surrenders Fort Morgan, after his magazines are threatened by Union bombardment—581 men surrender; 17 were killed in the bombardment.
September 1864	Forrest captures Athens, Alabama.

Date	Event(s)
fall 1864	Sherman twice orders the destruction of Cornwall Furnace during the Atlanta Campaign.
March 21–26, 1865	Raid of Union lieutenant colonel Andrew Spurling, from Milton, Florida, to Canoe Station, Alabama. The goal is to destroy the Alabama and Florida Railroad.
March 22, 1865	Wilson's Raid begins in Gravelly Springs in Lauderdale County, Alabama (northwest corner of the state).
March 27, 1865	Siege of Spanish Fort by Canby's forces begins.
March 29, 1865	Irondale Furnace is destroyed by the 4th Iowa during Wilson's Raid.
March 31, 1865	Confederate forces attack Wilson's cavalry at Montevallo, Alabama. Rolling mill, blast engine and boiler machinery at Shelby Iron Works are destroyed by troops under General Emory Upton (during Wilson's Raid). 8th Iowa Cavalry under Captain William A. Sutherland destroys the ironworks at Tannehill as part of Wilson's Raid. 10th Missouri Cavalry, commanded by Colonel Fredrick Bentee, destroys the Bibb works.
April 1, 1865	Battle of Ebenezer Church, (near Plantersville), Alabama; Forrest kills Union captain James D.M. Taylor (the last person Forrest killed in the Civil War).
April 2, 1865	Battle of Selma (Alabama)—Forrest defeated (and wounded). Siege of Fort Blakeley begins.
April 3, 1865	Selma Ordnance and Naval Foundry destroyed after Major General James Wilson takes the city.
April 4, 1865	Wilson's forces burn the University of Alabama at Tuscaloosa (a military school).

Date	Event(s)
April 8, 1865	Spanish Fort falls to forces under Canby.
April 9, 1865	Fort Blakeley falls to forces under Steele and Canby.
April 12, 1865	Wilson occupies Montgomery, Alabama. Mayor R.H. Slough surrenders the city of Mobile.
April 15, 1865	Tuskegee surrenders to Wilson's forces.
April 16, 1865	Forces under James Wilson capture Columbus, Georgia, and Fort Tyler (West Point), Georgia.
April 17–29, 1865	Raid of Union major general Benjamin Grierson, from Blakeley to Eufaula.
May 8, 1865	Forces under General Richard Taylor surrender in Citronelle, Alabama, to Major General Edward Canby.
May 9, 1865	Forrest surrenders in Gainesville, Alabama.
May 11, 1865	Lieutenant Colonel Milus E. "Bushwhacker" Johnston surrenders to Union colonel William Given at Trough Springs, Alabama.

Chapter 3

Capital of the Confederacy

Montgomery, Alabama, was an impressive city at the dawn of the Civil War, as this 1902 passage indicates:

> *In 1860 no city in the world gave back a sunnier smile in answer to the greetings of prosperity than Montgomery. All went well. Her people were rich and growing richer. In the main, they looked back to a proud ancestry in the older States, and they were building here in Alabama another centre where the graces of social life, the culture of mind and the standards of character were perpetuating the best traditions of the old South. They were ambitious and they were successful. They furnished to the drawing rooms of two continents women whose beauty and intellect won recognition everywhere. They supplied the noblest minds and the loftiest purposes to the brilliant galaxy of men who then guided the State and country. They could boast of men who were equally at home in politics and society and business, for among them were great developers, builders of factories and railroads and commerce, as well as the subduers of the forests. The spirit of help, of charity was everywhere. Want was unknown, for to suspect its approach was to relieve it in advance.*[32]

For several months in early 1861, Montgomery, Alabama, served as the capital of the Confederacy. It was here where the Provisional Confederate Congress named Jefferson Davis as the provisional president of the

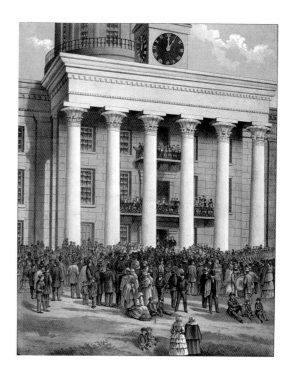

Right: Jefferson Davis is announced as president of the Confederacy in Montgomery, Alabama. *Courtesy of the Library of Congress.*

Below: First White House of the Confederacy, Montgomery. *Courtesy of the Library of Congress.*

Confederacy. His inauguration occurred on February 18, 1861. "Dixie" was played at the inauguration, and it quickly became one of the most popular songs in the Confederacy.

Date	Event(s)
1819	Montgomery, Alabama, is founded.
1846	Montgomery is named capital of Alabama.
February 1861	The Provisional Confederate Congress authorizes the leasing of an executive mansion.
February 9, 1861	Constitutional Convention in Montgomery, Alabama, considers Davis, Robert Toombs, Howell Cobb and Alexander Stephens for the presidency.
February 18, 1861	Davis is inaugurated as provisional president of the Confederacy.
March 1, 1861	Davis puts General P.G.T. Beauregard in charge of troops in the Charleston, South Carolina area.
May 21, 1861	Confederate Congress approves the move of the capital to Richmond, Virginia.
February 22, 1862	Davis is inaugurated as president of the Confederacy.
1974	First White House of the Confederacy is listed in the National Register of Historic Places.

As the end of winter turned into spring, and the heat and mosquito population rose, delegates to the Confederate Congress began to talk in animated tones about moving the capital to Richmond. Various reasons were given, including the location of the Tredegar Iron Works; its proximity to Washington, D.C.; and the prestige of having the capital in the state of Washington, Madison and Jefferson. But the real reason, according to diarist Mary Chesnut, was probably the comfort of the members of Congress:

Alabama State Capitol, Dexter Avenue, Montgomery. *Courtesy of the Library of Congress.*

We [Mary Chesnut and Varina Davis] *talked of this move from Montgomery. Mr. Chesnut opposes it violently, because this is so central a position for our government....I see that the uncomfortable hotels here will at last move the Congress. Our statesmen love their ease, and it will be hot here in summer.* "I do hope they will go," *Mrs. Davis said.* "The Yankees will make it hot for us, go where we will, and truly so if war comes." "And it has come," *said I.* "Yes, I fancy these dainty folks may live to regret losing even the fare of the Montgomery hotels." "Never."[33]

On May 21, 1861, the Confederate Congress approved the move of the capital to Richmond, Virginia.

Several years ago, I was giving a lecture in Montgomery to a SCV group, and the topic was "Why the South Lost the Civil War." In addition to the typical discussion of the North's advantage in resources (people and otherwise), the standardized railroad system in the North and the impact of the blockade, one gentleman in the audience stated, "The South lost the war the day they left Montgomery and moved the capital to Richmond." A case can be made for this statement. Much of the war on the part of the Confederacy was spent guarding Richmond from various Union threats

(McClellan in the Peninsula Campaign, the Dahlgren Raid, Petersburg and so on). Montgomery, much more remote from the point of view of Washington, D.C., would have presented a much more difficult (although not impossible) objective for Union attack.

WHAT IS LEFT TO SEE

- First White House of the Confederacy (644 Washington Avenue, Montgomery, AL, 36130)
- Alabama State Capitol (600 Dexter Avenue, Montgomery, AL, 36130)

Chapter 4

Battles

Timberclad Raid into Northern Alabama

After the fall of Fort Henry on February 6, 1862, Admiral Andrew Hull Foote sent the three "timberclad" gunboats (*Tyler*, *Conestoga* and *Lexington*) on a successful raid deep into Confederate territory, reaching as far as Muscle Shoals (Florence), Alabama. Among their targets was a bridge of the Memphis and Ohio Railroad, which was destroyed. Also captured or destroyed were Southern ships *Sallie Wood*, *Muscle* and *Eastport* (the latter was an ironclad under construction).

The commander of the expedition, Lieutenant S.L. Phelps, recounted the expedition in his report:

> *At night on the 7th we arrived at a landing in Hardin County, Tenn., known as Cerro Gordo, where we found the steamer* Eastport *being converted to a gunboat. Armed boats crews were immediately sent on board and search made for means of destruction that might have been devised. She had been scuttled and the suction pipes broken. These leaks were soon stopped. A number of rifle shots were fired at our vessels, but a couple of shells dispersed the rebels. On examination I found that there were large quantities of timber and lumber prepared for fitting up the* Eastport; *that the vessel itself, some 280 feet long, was in excellent condition and already half finished; considerable of the plating*

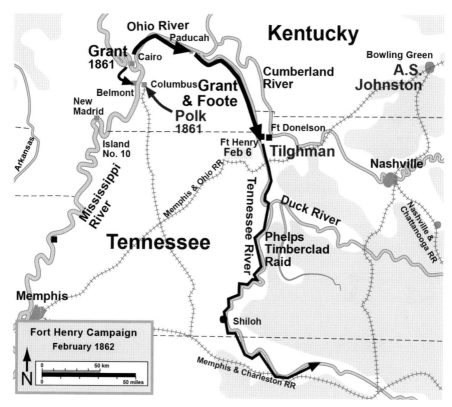

Above: This map of the Fort Henry Campaign (February 1862) shows how far south the Timberclad Raid went. *Creative Commons Attribution 3.0 Unported license. Map by Hal Jespersen, www.posix.com/CW.*

Right: Lieutenant Commander S.L. Phelps. *Courtesy of the Library of Congress.*

designed for her was lying on the bank and everything at hand to complete her. I therefore directed Lieutenant Commanding Gwin to remain with the Tyler to guard the prize, and to load the lumber, etc., while the Lexington and Conestoga should proceed still higher up.

Soon after daylight on the 8th we passed Eastport, Miss., and at Chickasaw, farther up, near the State line, seized two steamers, the Sallie Wood *and* Muscle; *the former laid up and the latter freighted with iron destined for Richmond and for rebel use. We then proceeded on up the river, entering the State of Alabama and ascending to Florence, at the foot of the Mussel Shoals. On coming in sight of the town three steamers were discovered, which were immediately set on fire by the rebels. Some shots were fired from the opposite side of the river below. A force was landed and considerable quantities of supplies, marked Fort Henry, were secured from the burning wrecks. Some had been landed and stored. These I seized, putting such as we could bring away on board our vessels and destroying the remainder. No flats or other craft could be found. I found also more of the iron and plating intended for the* Eastport [a steamer being converted to a gunboat in Hardin County, Tennessee].

A deputation of citizens of Florence waited upon me, first desiring that they might be made able to quiet the fears of their wives and daughters with assurances from me that they would not be molested; and, secondly, praying that I would not destroy their railroad bridge. As for the first I told them we were neither ruffians nor savages, and that we were there to protect from violence and to enforce the law; and with reference to the second, that if the bridge were away we could ascend no higher, and that it could possess, so far as I saw, no military importance, as it simply connected Florence itself with the railroad on the south bank of the river.

We had seized three of their steamers, one the half-finished gun-boat, and had forced the rebels to burn six others loaded with supplies, and their loss, with that of the freight, is a heavy blow to the enemy. Two boats are still known to be on the Tennessee, and are doubtless hidden in some of the creeks, where we shall be able to find them when there is time for the search…

S.L. Phelps, Lieutenant,
Commanding, U.S. Navy.

Flag-Officer, A.H. Foote, U.S. Navy,
Commanding Naval Forces, Western Waters.[34]

Mitchell Takes Huntsville

Shortly after the Timberclad Raid, Brigadier General Ormsby M. Mitchel launched an attack on northern Alabama, taking Huntsville on April

11, 1862. Among other stores and supplies, Mitchel captured sixteen (or seventeen) locomotives and one hundred railroad cars.

In a fairly innovative move for the time, Mitchel used the Memphis and Charleston Railroad to send troops east to Bridgeport and Stevenson and west to Athens and Decatur. Thus, he cut about a 150-mile swathe across northern Alabama. After taking Huntsville, Mitchel issued an order to his men:

> *Marching with a celerity such as to outstrip any messenger who might have attempted to announce your coming, you fell upon Huntsville, taking your enemy completely by surprise, and capturing not only his great military road, but all his machine-shops and rolling stock. Thus providing yourselves with ample transportation, you have struck blow after blow with a rapidity unparalleled. Stevenson fell, sixty miles to the east of Huntsville. Decatur and Tuscumbia have been in like manner seized, and are now occupied. In three days you have extended your front of operations more than one hundred and twenty miles, and your morning gun at Tuscumbia may now be heard by your comrades on the battle field made glorious by the victory before Corinth. A communication of these facts to headquarters has not only now the thanks of our commanding general, but those of the Department of War, which I announce to you with proud satisfaction. Accept the thanks of your commander, and let your future deeds demonstrate that you can surpass yourselves.*
>
> *By order of Gen. O.M. Mitchel.*[35]

The "Great Locomotive Chase" (or the Andrews Raid) was hatched as part of the operation of Mitchel's invasion, which was supposed to take Chattanooga after taking Huntsville. Mitchel never took Chattanooga, and for a variety of reasons (including heavy rain, which kept the raiders from burning bridges), the Andrews Raid failed on April 12, 1862.

Following are two newspaper accounts of Mitchel's successful invasion of northern Alabama:

> *A Chattanooga correspondent of the Augusta* Chronicle, *in a letter dated 16th instant, says:*
> *You have, of course, heard of the decent* [sic] *upon Huntsville by the Federal on Thursday last, their taking possession of the town and railroad, and also capturing a passenger train, together with the passengers.*
>
> *Two of the train hands from the Memphis and Charleston railroad arrived here today, having made their way from Huntsville, which they left*

Left: "Portrait of Brig. Gen. Ormsby M. Mitchel, officer of the Federal Army." *Courtesy of the Library of Congress.*

Below: This 1863 photo shows the railroad bridge across the Tennessee River at Bridgeport, Alabama. *Courtesy of the Library of Congress.*

on Sunday, the 13th. From them I learn that the Federalists have released the passengers that were captured on board the train, and have given them passports to leave.

On Saturday last there were 7,000 Federal troops at Huntsville. On Sunday, 5,000 were sent to Decatur and Corinth, while an additional force of 10,000 were expected to reach Huntsville on Monday. The Federalists captured eleven engines and a large number of cars, and pressed the Superintendent of the road, and all the engineers and train hands into service. They gave orders to run the trains as usual between the points occupied by them, and to collect the usual fares. They have already commenced running a daily mail to Huntsville, and are doing quite a driving business on their own account.[36]

Huntsville, Alabama, the town just occupied by Gen. Mitchell, is the capitol of Madison county, Ala., being 150 miles northeast of Tuscaloosa, and 116 miles southeast of Nashville. Its population in 1860 was about 5,000. Ex-Senator C.C. Clay resides there. In the summer months the cream of the Alabama aristocracy from the Gulf counties frequent the place. It is situated on the Memphis & Charleston Railroad, and by its occupation communication between the two rebel armies in the southwestern States is out.

The people generally may be classed as "conditional Unionists." Madison county, in which it is situated, has a population of 26,450, of whom 14,573 were slaves. At the last election it gave Douglas 1,300, Breckinridge 591, and Bell 400 votes.

In addition to Huntsville, Alabama, Gen. Mitchell has occupied Decatur, Monroe county, and Stevenson's Junction, Jackson county, in the same State. The former is thirty miles west southwest of Huntsville, on the Memphis and Charleston Railroad. The latter place is the junction of the Nashville & Chattanooga and Memphis & Charleston roads, and is sixty miles from Huntsville.[37]

ABEL STREIGHT'S RAID

In April 1863, Colonel Abel Streight received permission from General William Rosecrans to launch a cavalry raid on northern Alabama, parts of which had been under Union occupation since 1862. The ultimate goal was to disrupt operations on the Western and Atlantic Railroad in northeast Georgia, which

Emma Sansom monument on the west side of the Broad Street Bridge, Gadsden, Alabama. *Author's collection.*

was supplying Braxton Bragg's forces in Tennessee. Rosecrans approved of the plan, and Streight left Nashville in early April for Alabama.

There are certain "the gang that couldn't shoot straight"[38] aspects to this raid. Streight had assumed that he would be given horses for the raid, but instead he was given mules. Confederate sympathizers along the route of the raid ridiculed the Union force as they rode by on the ill-tempered mules. It is said that Forrest's cavalry could hear the *eee-aww* of the mules up to two miles away, making scouting efforts easy.

Later on in the raid, most of the ammunition of the 1,700-man force was ruined when it got wet crossing Will's Creek near Gadsden. Part of Streight's force was so tired from the march (and dealing with the mules) that they actually fell asleep during the final battle at Cedar Bluff, Alabama.

From Day's Gap in Cullman County (April 30) until the end of the raid, a much smaller force under Nathan Bedford Forrest (perhaps five hundred in total) kept up a constant harassment of Streight's troops. The first attack came at Day's Gap, which is probably the only skirmish that can really be considered a Union victory on the raid. Following is an excerpt from Streight's official report of the incident:

> We marched the next day (the 29th) to Day's Gap, about 35 miles, and bivouacked for the night....We moved out the next morning before daylight....I had not proceeded more than 2 miles, at the head of the column, before I was

informed that the rear guard had been attacked, and just at that moment I heard the boom of artillery in the rear of the column. I had previously learned that the gap through which we were passing was easily flanked by gaps through the mountains, both above and below; consequently I sent orders to the rear to hold the enemy in check until we could prepare for action. The head of the column was at the time on the top of the mountain. The column was moving through the gap; consequently the enemy was easily held in check. I soon learned that the enemy had moved through the gaps on my right and left, and were endeavoring to form a junction in my advance; consequently I moved ahead rapidly until we passed the intersecting roads on either

"Col. Abel D. Streight, 51ˢᵗ Ind. Inf. USA." *Courtesy of the Library of Congress.*

flank with the one we occupied. The country was open, sand ridges, very thinly wooded, and afforded fine defensive positions. As soon as we passed the point above designated (about 3 miles from the top of the mountains), we dismounted and formed a line of battle on a ridge circling to the rear. Our right rested on a precipitous ravine and the left was protected by a marshy run that was easily held against the enemy. The mules were sent into a ravine to the rear of our right, where they were protected from the enemy's bullets. I also deployed a line of skirmishers, resting on our right and left flanks encircling our rear, in order to prevent a surprise from any detached force of the enemy that might approach us from that direction and to prevent any straggling of either stray animals or cowardly men. In the mean time I had instructed Captain Smith, who had command of our rear guard (now changed to our front), to hold his position until the enemy pressed him closely, when he should retreat *rapidly, and, if possible, draw them on to our lines, which were concealed by the men lying down immediately back of the top of the ridge. The lines were left sufficiently open to permit Captain Smith's command to pass through near the center. I had two 12 pounder mountain howitzers, which were stationed near the road (the center). They were also concealed. We had hardly completed our arrangements when the enemy charged Captain Smith in large force, following him closely, and no sooner had he passed our lines than our whole line rose up and delivered a volley at short range. We continued to pour a rapid fire into their ranks, which soon caused them to give way in confusion; but their re-enforcements soon came up, when they dismounted, formed, and made a determined and vigorous attack. Our skirmishers were soon driven in, and about the same time the enemy opened upon us with a battery off artillery. The enemy soon attempted to carry our lines, but were handsomely repulsed. During their advance they had run their artillery to within 300 yards of our lines, and as soon as they began to waver I prepared for a charge. I ordered Colonel Hathaway, Seventy-third Indiana, and Lieutenant Colonel Sheets, Fifty-first Indiana, on the left, to make a charge, in order to draw the attention of the battery, and immediately threw the Third Ohio, Colonel Lawson, and the Eightieth Illinois, Lieutenant-Colonel Rodgers, forward*

John Wisdom monument—located about one hundred feet from the Emma Sansom monument in Gadsden. Wisdom rode sixty-seven miles to Rome, Georgia, to warn them that Streight's force was in Gadsden. *Author's collection.*

rapidly, hoping to capture the battery. The enemy, after a short but stubborn resistance, fled in confusion, leaving two pieces of artillery, two caissons, and about 40 prisoners, representing seven regiments, a large number of wounded, and about 30 dead on the field. Among the former was Captain [William H.] Forrest, a brother General Forrest. Our loss was about 30 killed and wounded, among the latter Lieutenant-Colonel Sheets.[39]

On May 2, 1863, Streight's forces reached the outskirts of Gadsden. After crossing Black Creek in Gadsden, Streight ordered the bridge burned to slow down the pursuit of Forrest. When Forrest saw the ruined bridge, he quickly rode to a nearby farm, where sixteen-year-old Emma Sansom offered to show him where she had seen some cows cross the Creek a few days before. Pulling her up behind him on the saddle, she showed him the fordable spot, and Forrest was soon in pursuit of Streight again.

Ferry operator (Coosa River) John Wisdom, whose ferry had been destroyed by Streight's forces, made a Paul Revere–style ride sixty-seven miles to Rome, Georgia, to tell them that Streight's force was in

Emma Sansom behind Nathan Bedford Forrest. *Author's collection.*

Gadsden. Rome then dispatched a small force to assist Forrest in his pursuit of Streight.

Some of the events in and around Gadsden and nearby Blount's Plantation are described in Streight's report (emphasis added):

I had learned in the mean time, through my scouts, that a large column of the enemy was moving on our left, parallel with our route, evidently with the intention of getting in our front, which made it necessary for us to march all night, though the command was in no condition to do so, and, to add still more to my embarrassment, a portion of our ammunition had become damaged in crossing will's creek, *which, at the time, was very deep fording. I only halted at Gadsden sufficiently long to destroy a quantity of arms and commissary stores found there, and proceeded on. Many of our animals and men were entirely worn out and unable to keep up with the column; consequently they fell behind the rear guard and were captured. It now became evident to me that our only hope was in crossing the river at Rome and destroying the bridge, which would delay Forrest a day or two and give us time to collect horses and mules, and allow the command a little time to sleep, without which it was impossible to proceed. The enemy followed closely, and kept up a continuous skirmish with the rear of the column until about 4 p.m., at which time we reached Blount's plantation, about 15 miles from Gadsden, where we could procure forage for our animals. Here I decided to halt, as it was impossible to continue the march through the night without feeding and resting, although to do so was to bring on a general engagement. Accordingly, the command was dismounted, and a detail made to feed the horses, and mules, while the balance of the command formed in line of battle on a ridge southwest of the plantation. Meanwhile the rear guard, in holding the enemy in check, had become severely engaged and was driven in. The enemy at once attacked our main line, and tried hard to carry the center, but were gallantly met and repulsed by the Fifty-first and Seventy-third Indiana, assisted by Major Vananda, with two mountain howitzers. They then made a determined effort to turn our right, but were met by the gallant Eightieth Illinois, assisted by two companies of the Third Ohio. The enemy, with the exception of a few skirmishers, then fell back to a ridge some half a mile distant, and commenced massing his force, as if preparing for a more determined attack. It was becoming dark, and I decided to withdraw unobserved, if possible, and conceal my command in a thicket some half a mile to our rear, there to lie in ambush and await his advance. In the mean time I had ordered Capt.*

Monument at the location outside Cedar Bluff where Abel Streight surrendered to Nathan Bedford Forrest. *Author's collection.*

Milton Russell (Fifty-first Indiana) to take 200 of the best mounted men, selected from the whole command, and proceed to Rome, and hold the bridge until the main command could come up. The engagement at Blount's Plantation revealed the fact that nearly all of our remaining ammunition was worthless, on account of having been wet. Much of that carried by the men had become useless by the paper wearing out and the powder sifting away.[40]

Streight's men were exhausted by this point, and many of the mules were dead or not usable. Streight figured that his only chance was to get to Rome and make a defense against Forrest's force there. However, he soon learned that part of Forrest's force was already ahead of him, heading toward Rome. The end came at Cedar Bluff, where, after a brief battle, Forrest and Streight discussed terms of surrender. During the surrender talks, Forrest kept part of his force moving in circles to make it seem much larger than it really was. Even with all of Streight's problems—wet ammunition, exhausted men, lack of transportation and more—he still outnumbered Forrest about 1,700 to 500. After the surrender, when Streight saw how small Forrest's force actually was, he was dismayed and wanted a do-over. Forrest responded with something along the lines of, "All is fair in love or war." Streight and his officers were shipped to Libby Prison, where Streight and some of them escaped on February 9, 1864. Streight wrote about his capture in his official report:

> *I was informed that a heavy force of the enemy was moving on our left, on a route parallel with the one we were marching, and was then nearer Rome than we were. About the same time I received this information our pickets were driven in. The command was immediately ordered into line, and every effort made to rally the men for action, but nature was exhausted, and* a large portion of my best troops actually went to sleep while lying in line of battle under a severe skirmish fire. *After some maneuvering, Forrest sent in a flag of truce, demanding the surrender of my forces. Most of my regimental commanders had already expressed the opinion that, unless we could reach Rome and cross the river before the enemy came up with us again, we should be compelled to surrender. Consequently I called a council of war. I had learned, however, in the mean time, that Captain Russell had been unable to take the bridge at Rome. Our condition was fully canvassed. As I have remarked before, our ammunition was worthless, our horses and mules in a desperate condition, the men were overcome with fatigue and loss of sleep, and we were confronted by fully three times our number…in the heart of the enemy's country, and although personally opposed to surrender, and so expressed myself at the time, yet I yielded to the unanimous voice of my regimental commanders, and at once entered into negotiations with Forrest to obtain the best possible terms I could for my command, and at about noon, May 3, we surrendered as prisoners of war. We were taken to Richmond, Va.*[41]

Several miscalculations were made that helped lead to the disaster of Streight's Raid, most prominent being an overestimation of the number of Union sympathizers in northern Alabama. While Streight did receive some help from the populace along the way, it was not of the size or scope that he had anticipated. A constant overestimation of the size of Forrest's force was an almost equal impediment to the success of the raid.

Date	Event(s)
July 1862	Colonel Abel Streight is part of the Federal occupation force in northern Alabama.

Date	Event(s)
April 24, 1863	Starting out in Nashville, Colonel Abel Streight's force of 1,700 reaches Tuscumbia, Alabama, at 5:00 p.m., where it joins with a force under Grenville Dodge.
April 30, 1863	Battle of Day's Gap (Cullman County)—casualties, Union: 23; Confederate: 65 Skirmishes at Crooked Creek and Hog Mountain.
May 1, 1863	Skirmishes at Blountsville and the Black Warrior River (East Branch).
May 2, 1863	Skirmishes near Gadsden, Alabama, and Blount's plantation. Sixteen-year-old Emma Sansom rides behind Nathan Bedford Forrest to show him where he could ford Black Creek. Streight had burned the only bridge shortly before. Ferry operator (Coosa River) John Wisdom rides sixty-seven miles to Rome, Georgia, to tell them that Streight's force is in Gadsden. Rome sends a small force to assist Forrest in his pursuit of Streight.
May 3, 1863	Battle of Cedar Bluff, Alabama, where Abel Streight is captured by Nathan Bedford Forrest. Streight will be sent to Libby Prison.
February 9, 1864	Streight and some of his men participate in the great prison escape from Libby Prison.
1906	Gadsden erects a monument to Emma Sansom.

BATTLE OF MOBILE BAY

Never did people fight their vessels to more effect than did Farragut and his officers on this occasion. The battle was short and decisive; and although the Confederates claim that their vessels fought desperately from 7 o'clock until 10, the truth is that the last encounter between the ram and the fleet only lasted from 8.50 until 10 o'clock, one hour and ten minutes. Hours and minutes fly fast when under fire and amid the excitement there were incidents enough in this battle to make time pass rapidly.[42]

−*David Dixon Porter*

	Union	**Confederate**
Casualties[43]	322	1,500
Commanders	Gordon Granger David Farragut	Richard Lucian Page Admiral Franklin Buchanan
Date	August 5, 1864	
Outcome	Union victory	

In 1864, Mobile Bay was the last port the Confederacy had on the Gulf of Mexico. Rear Admiral David G. Farragut attacked the Confederate fleet there on August 5, 1864, while a contingent of Union soldiers under Major General Gordon Granger attacked the three forts that guarded the bay: Powell, Gaines and Morgan.

"Great naval victory in Mobile Bay, Aug. 5th 1864." *Courtesy of the Library of Congress.*

Date	Event(s)
1821	Fort Gaines is constructed.
1834	Fort Morgan (masonry) is constructed.
April 1862	Mobile Bay becomes the only defensible port on the gulf for the Confederacy.
September 4, 1862	CSS *Florida* runs the U.S. Navy blockade into Mobile Bay.
January 15, 1863	CSS *Florida* runs the U.S. Navy blockade out of Mobile Bay.
May 18, 1864	Confederate ironclad *Tennessee* (with six guns) enters the bay.
August 3, 1864	About 1,500 Union troops are stationed west of Fort Gaines, preparing for an assault. By the next day, they are dug in half a mile from the fort.
August 5, 1864	Battle of Mobile Bay; Fort Powell is abandoned on orders from Lieutenant Colonel Williams.
August 8, 1864	Fort Gaines is surrendered by Colonel Charles D. Anderson.
August 23, 1864	Brigadier General Richard L. Page surrenders Fort Morgan after his magazines are threatened by Union bombardment.

The Confederate fleet comprised four ships, but only one really mattered. There were three side-wheel gunboats: CSS *Selma*, CSS *Morgan* and CSS *Gaines*. The ironclad CSS *Tennessee* served as the flagship of Admiral Franklin Buchanan.

The Union fleet comprised fourteen wooden-hulled ships and four ironclads. The wooden-hulled ships were lashed together two-by-two as they sailed into the bar. *Hartford* was the flagship.

Ship	Commander	Notes	Casualties
(1) *Brooklyn*	Captain James Alden	wooden-hulled	54
(1) *Octorara*	Lieutenant Commander C.H. Greene	double-ended side-wheeler	11

"Admiral Farragut and Captain Drayton on deck of U.S. frigate Hartford." *Courtesy of the Library of Congress.*

Ship	Commander	Notes	Casualties
(2) *Hartford*	Captain Percival Drayton	wooden-hulled, flagship	53
(2) *Metacomet*	Lieutenant Commander James E. Jouett	double-ended side-wheeler	3
(3) *Richmond*	Captain Thornton A. Jenkins	wooden-hulled	2
(3) *Port Royal*	Lieutenant Commander Bancroft Gherardi	double-ended side-wheeler	
(4) *Lackawanna*	Captain J.B. Marchand	wooden-hulled	39

Ship	Commander	Notes	Casualties
(4) *Seminole*	Commander E. Donaldson	wooden-hulled	
(5) *Monongahela*	Commander J.H. Strong	wooden-hulled	6
(5) *Kennebec*	Lieutenant Commander W.P. McCann	gunboat	7
(6) *Ossipee*	Commander Wm. E. LeRoy	wooden-hulled	8
(6) *Itasca*	Commander George Brown	gunboat	
(7) *Oneida*	Commander J.R.M. Mullany	wooden-hulled	38
(7) *Galena*	Lieutenant Commander C.H. Wells	wooden-hulled	1
Tecumseh	Commander T.A.M. Craven	ironclad, already inside the bar	93
Manhattan	Commander J.W.A. Nicholson	ironclad, already inside the bar	
Winnebago	Commander T.H Stevens	ironclad, already inside the bar	
Chickasaw	Lieutenant Commander George H. Perkins	ironclad, already inside the bar	
Total killed: 145; total wounded: 170			

The Union fleet sustained heavy fire from Forts Morgan and Gaines. During this fire, the USS *Tecumseh* had hit a mine ("torpedo" in Civil War parlance). Farragut shouted through a sound trumpet something along the lines of, "Damn the torpedoes, full speed ahead!" After the Civil War, Farragut's brother David Dixon Porter told the story:

It was apparent to Farragut that there was some difficulty ahead, and that the advance of the fleet was arrested, while Fort Morgan was firing with great effect upon the stationary vessels. At this moment the Admiral also witnessed the sinking of the "Tecumseh," with nearly all her officers and crew. It was an appalling spectacle, and would have daunted many other men. He did not know but that his whole fleet would be blown up in less than a minute, and their hulls and guns lying at the bottom of the bay. He did not hesitate, however, but gave the order to Captain Drayton: "Pass the 'Brooklyn,' and take the lead." His order was immediately obeyed, and as the flag-ship went by him, Captain Alden informed the Admiral that he was "running into a nest of torpedoes." "D--n the torpedoes," he replied, "follow me!" At the same time he directed the commander of the "Metacomet" to send a boat and pick up any of the "Tecumseh's" survivors that he could find.[44]

Farragut's son, Loyall Farragut, in his book, *The Life of David Glasgow Farragut, First Admiral of the United States Navy*, recounted the famous scene somewhat differently:

By half past seven the Tecumseh *was well up with the fort, and drawing slowly by the* Tennessee, *having her on the port beam, when suddenly she reeled to port and went down with almost every soul on board, destroyed by a torpedo.*

Craven, in his eagerness to engage the ram, had passed to the west of the fatal buoy. If he had gone but his breadth of beam eastward of it, he would have been safe, so far as the torpedoes were concerned.

This appalling disaster was not immediately realized by the fleet. Some supposed the Tennessee *had been sunk, or some advantage gained over the enemy, and cheer after cheer from the* Hartford *was taken up and echoed along the line. But Farragut, from his lofty perch, saw the true state of affairs, and his anxiety was not decreased when the* Brooklyn, *just ahead, suddenly stopped. He hailed his pilot Freeman above him in the top, to ask, "What is the matter with the* Brooklyn? *She must have plenty of water there." "Plenty and to spare, Admiral," the man replied. Alden had seen the* Tecumseh *go down, and the heavy line of torpedoes across the channel made him pause. The* Brooklyn *began to back; the vessels in the rear, pressing on those in the van, soon created confusion, and disaster seemed imminent. "The batteries of our ships were almost silent," says an eye-witness, "while the whole of Mobile Point was a living flame."*

"What's the trouble?" was shouted through a trumpet from the flag-ship to the Brooklyn.

"Torpedoes!" was shouted back in reply.

"Damn the torpedoes!" said Farragut. "Four bells! Captain Drayton, go ahead! Jouett, full speed!" And the Hartford passed the Brooklyn, *assumed the head of the line, and led the fleet to victory. It was the only way out of the difficulty, and any hesitation would have closed even this escape from a frightful disaster. Nor did the Admiral forget the poor fellows who were struggling in the water where the* Tecumseh *has gone down, but ordered Jouett to lower a boat and pick up the survivors.*[45]

Once Farragut's fleet had broken through into the bay, Farragut turned his attention to the Confederate ironclad CSS *Tennessee*. Admiral Porter described the fight against the *Tennessee*:

The iron-clads, and such wooden vessels as had been prepared with iron prows, were ordered to attack the "Tennessee" at once, before she could reach

---

CSS *Tennessee*

- Acquisition: Built at Mobile, Alabama.
- Cost: $595,000.
- Description: Casemated ironclad.
- Tonnage: 1,273.
- Dimensions: Length, 209 feet; beam, 48 feet.
- Draft: August 13, 1864, average, 14 feet.
- Engines: Two, geared, noncondensing. Cylinders 24 inches in diameter, 84 inches stroke. Poppet valves, placed fore and aft; geared to idle shaft by spur gearing with wooden teeth and from idle shaft to propeller shaft by bevel cast iron gear.
- Boilers: Four, horizontal flue, 24 feet long, placed side by side with one furnace under all of them; one smoke pipe.
- Battery: August 13, 1864, 2 7.5-inch rifle pivots. 4.6-inch rifles in broadside.
- Disposition: Surrendered at Mobile to the Federals, August 5, 1864.[46]

---

the centre of the fleet, and the wooden vessels were directed to ram the iron-clad and attempt to disable her in that way.

Thus the fleet and the "Tennessee" were approaching each other rapidly, while the people in the former were watching keenly for the result, no one being able to form an opinion as to the power of the latter for offensive purposes, or what might be the plan of her commander, who was standing fearlessly on as if conscious that he was more than a match for the Federals. And now commenced one of the most remarkable combats known throughout the war—in fact, one of the fiercest naval battles on record.

The "Monongahela," Commander Strong, was the first vessel that had the honor of striking the "Tennessee," which she did squarely and fairly, with a

---

USS *Hartford*

- Acquisition: By government; machinery by Harrison Loring, Boston, Massachusetts. Launched on November 22, 1858, at Boston Navy Yard.
- Cost: $502,650.16.
- Description: Class, Screw steamer; first-class sloop; wood. Rate, rig, etc.: 2d; ship.
- Tonnage: 2,900.
- Dimensions: Length, 225 feet; beam, 44 feet; depth, 18 feet, 6 inches.
- Draft: Forward, 16 feet, 2 inches; aft, 17 feet, 2 inches.
- Speed: Maximum, 13.5 knots; average 8 knots.
- Engines: Two, horizontal, condensing, double piston rod. Diameter of cylinder, 62 inches; stroke, 34 inches.
- Boilers: Two, vertical, tubular (Martins patent); 1 small boiler, with 1 furnace.
- Battery: June 20, 1862, 20 9-inch Dahlgren S.B., 2 20-pounder. Parrott rifles, 1 heavy 12-pounder, 1 light 12-pounder; June 9, 1863, 1 45-pounder Sawyer rifle, 2 30-pounder Parrott rifles, 24 9-inch Dahlgren S.B.; March 31, 1864, 2 100-pounder Parrott rifles, 1 30-pounder Parrott rifle, 18 9-inch Dahlgren S.B.; June 23, 1864, add 3 12-pounder howitzers.
- Disposition: Still in the service at Charleston, South Carolina.
- Remarks: Commenced in December 1857 and completed in June 1859.[47]

good head of steam; but the only result was that the ramming vessel carried away her cast-iron prow, together with the cut-water,[48] *without apparently doing the "Tennessee" any damage. Just afterwards, the "Lackawanna," Captain Marchand, delivered a blow, going at full speed, crushing in her own stem, but had no other effect on the ram than to give her a heavy list. The Admiral then dashed at his enemy with the "Hartford," but only got in a glancing blow, for the "Tennessee" avoided his attack by shifting her helm*

"Farragut's flagship Hartford." *Courtesy of the Library of Congress.*

in time. The flag ship rasped alongside of her and delivered a broadside from her starboard guns as she passed, but with little or no effect.

This was a reception Buchanan did not anticipate. He had calculated on catching the fleet in confusion, and expected to enact again the role of the "Albemarle" [sunk on October 27, 1864] in the Sounds of North Carolina. But here the conditions were quite different. The rattling of the 9-inch shot on the "Tennessee's" casements made his vessel fairly quiver, while the ramming demoralized her crew, they having been made to believe that no one would undertake such an adventure.

The Monitors were slow in speed, but they had now reached the "Tennessee's" wake, delivering their fire as opportunity offered. The "Manhattan," Commander J.W.A. Nicholson, got close under her stern and fired a raking shot (15-inch), which struck the "Tennessee's" port-quarter and carried away her steering gear. The "Manhattan" fired altogether six times, and most of her shots took effect. In the meantime, the "Winnebago" and "Chickasaw" were firing as opportunity offered. The smokestack of the "Tennessee" was shot away by the "Chickasaw," which vessel followed her closely, firing solid shot into her until her flag was hauled down.

If the commander of the ram had calculated that he could scatter the gallant officers who were swarming about him, he had reckoned without his host, for never did an iron-clad receive such a battering in so short a time. Every ship in the fleet tried to get alongside of her to throw in a broadside, but there was not room for all to manoeuvre; and the "Lackawanna." in her desire to have another blow at the enemy, collided with the "Hartford." and cut her down on the quarter to within two feet of the water line.

Meanwhile the "Tennessee" was not idle. All her guns were at work as fast as they could be loaded and fired. She was like a great buffalo of the plains, with a pack of wolves hanging to its flanks, finally compelled to succumb to superior numbers. But the ram managed to inflict some dreadful wounds in her last efforts.

While the "Hartford" was drifting by her, and from a distance of ten feet or less was pouring in a broadside of 9-inch solid shot, with charges of thirteen pounds of powder, without any effect, the "Tennessee" fired a large shell through her side, which burst on the berth-deck, killing and wounding a number of men, the pieces breaking through the spar and berth-decks, passing through the launch and entering the hold among the wounded. There was no time to think of the danger from shot or shell, for every one's blood was up, and it was determined that the "Tennessee" should not escape, if it cost the lives of every one in the fleet.

The "Hartford," after being struck by the "Lackawanna," was at first reported to be sinking; but that report was soon set at rest, and she started for the enemy at full speed, determined this time to crush in her side or be crushed in the attempt. But as the flag-ship approached the "Tennessee," it was seen that she was flying a white flag, so the former sheered off without delivering the intended blow.[49]

While the Union navy was winning in the bay, the Union army was doing its part against the forts. On August 3, 1864, two days before the great naval battle, 1,500 Union troops were stationed west of Fort Gaines, preparing for an assault. By the next day, they were dug in half a mile from the fort and began moving closer through a series of trenches. Fort Gaines was surrendered by Colonel Charles D. Anderson on August 8, 1864.

Meanwhile, on August 5, 1864, Fort Powell was abandoned on orders from Lieutenant Colonel Williams without a shot fired.

Fort Morgan, under Brigadier General Richard L. Page, lasted the longest. But it, too, surrendered on August 23, 1864, after the Union bombardment came close to exploding the fort's magazines.

"Confederate ram Tennessee, Mobile, Alabama." *Courtesy of the Library of Congress.*

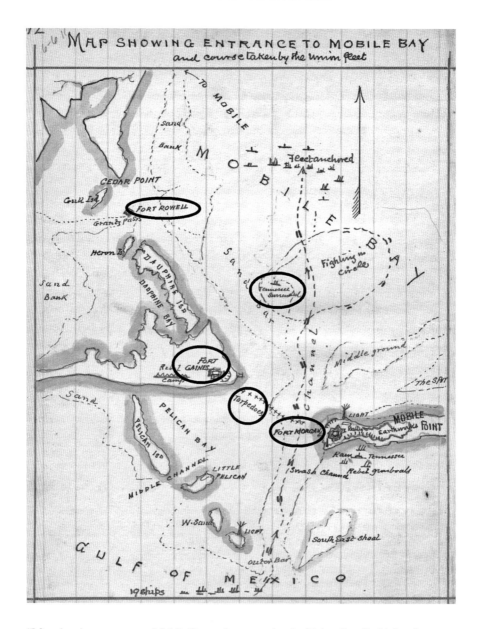

"Map showing entrance to Mobile Bay and course taken by Union fleet," with key features circled by the author. *Courtesy of the Library of Congress.*

The Battle of Mobile Bay was key on more than one level. First, the last Confederate port on the Gulf Coast had been shut down. Second, this battle turned out to be the death knell of the wooden ship. Farragut, who had long been an advocate of the wooden-hulled ship, readily admitted after the battle that the damage done to the wooden-hulled ships by the Confederate ironclad CSS *Tennessee* had been significant. Finally, Mobile Bay was the final fulfillment of the Anaconda Plan.

Farragut was promoted to vice-admiral on December 21, 1864, and to admiral on July 25, 1866. He died in 1870.

WILSON'S RAID

Major General James Wilson conducted a raid through Alabama and Georgia in March–May 1865, destroying Confederate factories, capturing Confederate armories and arsenals and capturing Selma, Alabama; Montgomery, Alabama; Columbus, Georgia; and West Point, Georgia.

Wilson was sent on the raid by Major General George "Rock of Chickamauga" Thomas, who had destroyed the army of John Bell Hood in November 1864. Under Wilson were divisions headed by Brigadier General Edward M. McCook, Brigadier General Eli Long and Brigadier General Emory Upton. The force amounted to 13,500. Much of the force was armed with seven-shot Spencer repeating rifles.

Opposing Wilson's force were about 2,500 cavalry under Nathan Bedford Forrest, plus various home guard and militia.

Date	Event(s)
March 20–22, 1865	Raid begins in Gravelly Springs in Lauderdale County, Alabama (northwest corner of the state). Wilson divides his forces into three columns.
March 25, 1865	Skirmish at Houston, Alabama.
March 26, 1865	Skirmish at Black Warrior River.
March 27, 1865	Columns rejoin at Jasper; county courthouse is burned.
March 28, 1865	Skirmish at Elyton (near modern Birmingham). Iron furnaces at Oxmoor and Irondale are destroyed.

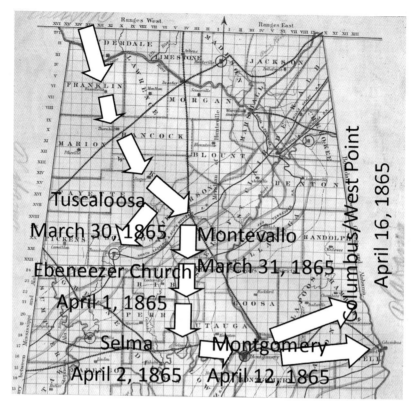

Route and dates of Wilson's Raid superimposed on an 1866 map of Alabama. *Courtesy of the Library of Congress.*

Date	Event(s)
March 29, 1865	Wilson briefly uses the the residence of Judge William S. Mudd as a headquarters. (Today, this site is the Arlington Antebellum Home and Gardens: Arlington Place, 331 Cotton Avenue Southwest, Birmingham, Alabama.)
March 30, 1865	Wilson sends Brigadier General John T. Croxton toward Tuscaloosa with 1,500 troops.
March 31, 1865	Wilson destroys Shelby Iron Works, Roupes Valley Ironworks at Tannehill and Bibb Naval Furnace at Brierfield. Forrest is beaten back at Montevallo, Alabama (south of Birmingham).

Date	Event(s)
	Forrest is defeated at Ebenezer Church (Stanton).
April 1, 1865	Skirmish at Trion (Tuscaloosa County) between Croxton's brigade and forces under Brigadier General Chalmers and Brigadier General Jackson.
April 2, 1865	Battle of Selma—Forrest defeated (and wounded).
April 4, 1865	Brigadier General John T. Croxton burns the University of Alabama at Tuscaloosa (a military school).
April 12, 1865	Wilson occupies Montgomery.
April 16, 1865	Battle of West Point—the Union takes Fort Tyler.
	Battle of Columbus—Wilson's forces take the city and destroy the Confederate ram CSS *Jackson*.
April 19, 1865	Destruction of the Mount Pinson Ironworks by Brigadier General John T. Croxton.
April 20, 1865	Macon, Georgia, surrenders, and Major General Howell Cobb and Major General Gustavus Smith are captured.
April 23, 1865	John Croxton defeats Benjamin Jefferson Hill in a skirmish at Munford, Alabama.

EBENEZER CHURCH/PLANTERSVILLE

The first major skirmish with Forrest during Wilson's Raid occurred on April 1 at Ebenezer Church, near Stanton, Alabama. Wilson had captured dispatches from Forrest to General Jackson, so by 9:00 a.m., Wilson had a good idea of the disposition of Forrest's forces. Wilson had close to 7,500 troops, while Forrest had only 1,500. Forrest killed his last man in the war in this battle: Union captain James D.M. Taylor.

Wilson discussed the captured dispatches in his official report:

> *April 1, moved at daylight. Upton, in advance, struck the rebels again at Randolph; drove them rapidly back. At 9 a.m. captured couriers with dispatches from Colonel Anderson, of Forrest's staff, to General Jackson,*

Ebenezer Church as it looks today, in downtown Stanton, Alabama. A historical marker describing the battle is on the right side of the picture. *Author's collection.*

by which I learned that Jacksons division had camped at Scottsville, on the Tuscaloosa and Centerville road, the night before, and that Croxton had reached Trion. Chalmers at Marion, Ala., but ordered to cross Cahawba and put his division between us and Selma. I immediately ordered McCook, with La Granges brigade, to march as rapidly as possible, seize the Centerville bridge, push on, form a junction with Croxton, and, if possible, break up Jacksons force and rejoin the corps by the Centerville and Selma road.

The other two divisions pursued the rebels, now known to be under Forrest in person; found them in position on the north bank of a creek at Ebenezer Station, five miles from Plantersville. General Longs advance regiment, the Seventeenth Indiana, of Millers brigade, made a gallant charge, capturing 1 gun and some prisoners, while Upton, with Alexander's brigade, struck them on the right flank, capturing 2 guns and about 300 prisoners. General Winslow's brigade followed up the advantage, pushing the rebels, now re-enforced by Armstrong's brigade, of Chalmers division, rapidly beyond Plantersville.

Detachments from the Fourth Cavalry destroyed railroad bridges from Montevallo down. Camped at Plantersville, twenty miles from Selma.[50]

SELMA, TUSCALOOSA AND MONTGOMERY

Nathan Bedford Forrest took command of the defenses in Selma on the morning of April 2, 1865. While he had almost four thousand men, many were militia (comprising old men and boys). There was not enough of them to adequately man the three miles of fortifications around Selma.

- 2:00 p.m.: Wilson's force arrived before the fortifications at Selma. He had about nine thousand men available.

- 3:00 p.m.: Confederate pickets driven in; Lieutenant General Richard Taylor left Selma by railroad.

- 5:00 p.m.: An ammunition train in Wilson's rear was attacked by members of Forrest's force still making their way to Selma. Brigadier General Eli Long's division attacked the Selma fortifications and broke through after vicious fighting, lasting about thirty minutes. Long was injured in the scalp during the assault. Major General Emory Upton's division attacked next, followed by a cavalry charge with Lieutenant O'Connell leading the 4th U.S. Cavalry Regiment. Eventually, the defenders were pushed back, first to the inner defenses of the fortifications and then to the railroad depot in Selma.

- 7:00 p.m.: The Confederate defenders were outflanked. Many hundreds were taken prisoners (Union: 359; Confederate: 2,700),

Ruins of the Selma Ordnance and Naval Foundry, April 1865.

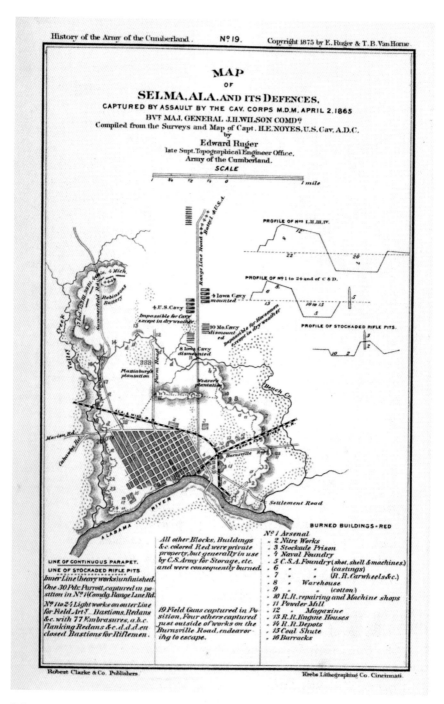

Selma, Alabama, and its defenses. *Courtesy of the Library of Congress.*

although many escaped, including Forrest, who retreated to Marion, Alabama (early newspaper reports reported that Forrest himself was captured, but this proved not to be true).

Wilson described the Battle of Selma in his official report:

April 2, marched at daylight, Long's division in advance. Approached city by Summersfield road, Upton's division on the Range Line road. Drove in pickets and closed in upon the defenses by 3 p.m. Having previously obtained detailed plans of the rebel works, made a hasty reconnaissance to ascertain the accuracy of the drawings. Directed General Long to attack on the right of the Summerfield road, whilst General Upton was to penetrate the swamps at a point regarded impassable by the enemy and attack just after dark. Before General Upton could get into position, Chalmers attached General Long's picket posted on the creek to cover his rear. Long, without waiting for the signal, with admirable judgment, immediately began the attack with two dismounted regiments from each brigade, 1,160 men in all, himself, Colonels Miller and Minty, gallantly leading their men. They charged 500 yards over an open and level field, leaping over and tearing up the stockade in front of the works, pushed through the ditch over the parapet, and swept everything before them. Armstrong's brigade, with nearly 1,500 men, defended that part of the line. General Long was severely wounded in the scalp; Colonels Miller, Seventy-second Indiana, and McCormick, Seventh Pennsylvania, through leg; Colonel Dobb, Fourth Ohio, was killed; Colonel Biggs was shot through the chest. Total loss, 46 killed, 200 wounded. As soon as an order could be got to General Upton, with his usual intrepidity he pushed his division forward, meeting but slight resistance, taking many prisoners. The rebels rallied behind the inner line of works, not yet finished. The Fourth U.S. Cavalry, Lieutenant O'Connell commanding, made a handsome charge, but could not penetrate the works. Rallied and dismounted under a withering fire of musketry; supported by the Seventeenth Indiana, Third Ohio, and Chicago Board of Trade Battery, they carried the inner line in handsome style. By this time it was quite dark, and in the confusion Generals Forrest, Adams, Buford, and Armstrong, with about half of their forces, escaped by the road toward Burnsville; Lieutenant-General Taylor had left at 3 p.m. on the cars. Two thousand seven hundred prisoners, including 150 officers, 26 field guns, and one 30-pounder Parrott in position, about 70 heavy guns, besides large quantities of military stores in the arsenal and foundry, fell into our hands and were destroyed; 25,000 bales of cotton were burned by the rebels.[51]

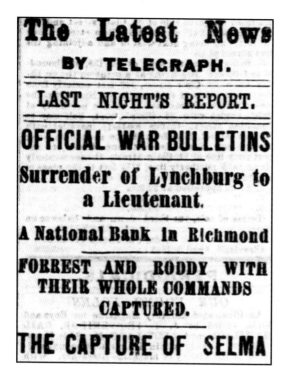

The Latest News
BY TELEGRAPH.
LAST NIGHT'S REPORT.
OFFICIAL WAR BULLETINS
Surrender of Lynchburg to a Lieutenant.
A National Bank in Richmond
FORREST AND RODDY WITH THEIR WHOLE COMMANDS CAPTURED.
THE CAPTURE OF SELMA

"The Capture of Selma." *From the* Cleveland Morning Leader, *April 13, 1865.*

Following are two excerpts from newspaper articles discussing the events at Selma:

The cotton warehouses, government works, and navy yard at Selma were burned by the Federals, and a few houses accidentally. General Forrest fought brilliantly, and was wounded three times, but did not leave the field....

In Selma all the cotton was burned, but little Government property was saved. The loss is many millions. The loss of the city is attributed to a disgraceful stampede. There were very few of Forrest's men in the fight as his command had not arrived in time to, meet the enemy's assault, which occurred on Saturday afternoon and continued for an hour very hard. The enemy suddenly charged our left on the West of Selma, where our line was weakest, and cast a few shell among-the horse-holders who stampeded. Our forces then retreated in confusion to Selma. Gens. Forrest and Adams boldly cut their way out towards Montgomery, but with some difficulty. Gen. Taylor left Demopolis the same evening, but before the fight began.[52]

On the 2d of April he [Wilson] captured Selma, Ala, by assault, taking 32 pieces of artillery In position and 75 In arsenal; a large arsenal, the second in importance in the Confederacy; a naval foundry, very extensive, with valuable fixtures, powder works, &c., &c. All public property was destroyed.

A pontoon bridge, 850 feet long, was built across the Alabama river, by which Montgomery was reached.[53]

On April 4, 1865, the University of Alabama at Tuscaloosa (a military school) was burned:

The command then moved on Tuscaloosa, arriving in front of the place about 10 p.m. of the 2d [third]. *A careful reconnaissance by General Croxton in person determined the fact that we were unexpected. The Second Michigan Cavalry, Col. T.W. Johnston commanding, was dismounted and thrown quietly forward toward the bridge. The six pickets on duty at the end approached were surprised and captured. The planks in the center of the bridge, however, had been taken up, and in relaying these the alarm was given. The column, however, was pushed forward sufficiently far to cover all approaches to the bridge and prevent its recapture. Farther advance was not made, owing to the fact that the enemy had opened a very rapid fire of musketry from behind cotton bales in the streets. During the night the garrison of 300 cadets and 200 armed citizens withdrew. Our loss in the fighting, twenty-three killed and wounded, all from the Second Michigan Cavalry. We captured Colonel Hardcastle, commanding the post, 9 other commissioned officers, and 63 enlisted men; also three 6-pounder guns in good condition. The enemys loss in killed and wounded not ascertained, but not supposed to be heavy.*

On the 3d [the fourth] *the university buildings, all the factories, machine-shops, together with a large amount of bacon, corn, harness, fifty-odd wagons and ambulances, were destroyed. All private property was respected, and the soldiers were not permitted to enter houses. On the morning of the 4th* [the fifth] *the command moved out of Tuscaloosa, crossed the bridge and burned it.*[54]

On April 12, 1865, Wilson occupied Montgomery:

Montgomery surrendered without assault. Five guns fell into our hands....We destroyed two rolling mills and foundries, two magazines; sixty-three cars, one locomotive; five steamboats were captured on the river near Wetumpka.[55]

Next, Wilson attacked West Point and Columbus Georgia, often considered the last battles of the Civil War.

WEST POINT/COLUMBUS

On April 16, 1865, Federal cavalry under Colonel Oscar Hugh La Grange captured Fort Tyler at West Point. It was the last capture of a fort in the war. On the same day, in a daring nighttime attack, forces under James H. Wilson stormed across the bridges and took Columbus, Georgia. The Confederate ironclad ram CSS *Jackson* was destroyed as part of the occupation of Columbus. These are often considered the final battles of the Civil War, as they occurred just before Johnston's surrender on April 26, 1865, in North Carolina. Technically, the Battle of Palmito Ranch in Texas occurred after the war was over (May 12–13, 1865).

The Battle of Fort Tyler involved Union cavalry laying down wooden bridges across a twelve-foot-wide ditch to storm the parapets. Federal sharpshooters laid down a withering fire from nearby houses. Confederate brigadier general Robert C. Tyler was killed in the fighting.

From 1897 to 1959, the site of Fort Tyler was used as a city reservoir. An archaeological team conducted a dig on the site in 1991 and found much of the original fort intact. It had actually been somewhat preserved because a portion of the fort had been under water for many years.

This article from the *Memphis Daily Appeal* describes the battle:

> *After much sharp skirmishing and hard marching, which resulted in the capture of fourteen wagons and a number of prisoners, La Grange's advance reached the vicinity of West Point at ten A.M., April sixteenth, with Beck's Eighteenth Indiana Battery and the Second and Fourth Indiana Cavalry. The enemy were kept occupied till the arrival of the balance of the Brigade. Having thoroughly reconnoitered the ground, detachments of the First Wisconsin, Second Indiana, and Seventh Kentucky Cavalry dismounted and prepared to assault Fort Tyler, covering the bridge. Col. La Grange describes it as a remarkably strong bastioned earthwork, thirty-five yards square, surrounded by a ditch twelve feet wide and ten feet deep, situated on a commanding eminence, protected by an imperfect* abbatis *and mounting two thirty-two pounders and two field guns.*
>
> *At one p.m. the charge was sounded and the brave detachment on the three sides of the work rushed forward to the assault, drove the rebel skirmishers into the fort, and followed under a withering fire of musketry and grape to the edge of the ditch. This was found impassable; but without falling back, Col. La Grange posted sharpshooters to keep down the enemy and organized parties to gather materials for the bridges. As soon*

as this had been done he sounded the charge again; the detachment sprang forward again, laid the bridges, and rushed forward over the parapet into the work, capturing the entire garrison—in all, two hundred and sixty-five men.[56] Gen. Tyler, its commanding officer, with eighteen men and officers killed, and twenty-eight severely wounded. Simultaneously with the advance upon the fort the Fourth Indiana dashed through the town, secured both bridges over the Chattahoochee, scattering a superior force of cavalry which had just arrived, and burned five engines and trains. Col. La Grange highly commends the accuracy and steadiness of Capt. Beck in the use of his artillery.…

Col. La Grange destroyed at this place two bridges, nineteen locomotives, and two hundred and forty-five cars loaded with quartermaster, commissary and ordnance stores. Before leaving he established a hospital for the wounded of both sides, and left with the Major an ample supply of stores to provide for all their wants.[57]

The attack on Columbus, Georgia, on the same day as Fort Tyler would have been considered one of the great victories of the war for the Union if it hadn't happened so late in the war. Essentially, three hundred men took Columbus in a nighttime attack. As was the case at Selma, Griswoldville, Allatoona and other battles, the Union use of repeating rifles (Spencer) was crucial:

Fort Tyler as it appears today. *Author's collection.*

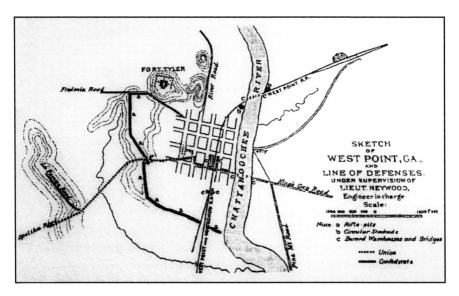

This Civil War–era map shows the relationship of Fort Tyler to the city of West Point and the Chattahoochee River (from a sign at the site). *Author's collection.*

Grave of Brigadier General Tyler (*left*). *Author's collection.*

About two p.m. of the sixteenth, Gen. Upton's advance-a part of Alexander's Brigade-struck the enemy's pickets on the road and drove them rapidly through Girard [now Phenix City] *to the lower bridge over the Chattahoochee at*

Columbus. The rebels hastily set fire to it, and thereby prevented its capture. After securing a position on the lower Montgomery Road, Gen. Upton detached a force to push around to the bridge or the factory, three miles above the city. He then made a reconnaissance in person and found the enemy strongly posted in a line of works covering all the bridges with a large number of guns in position on both sides of the river. He had already determined to move Winslow's Brigade to the Opelika or Summerville Road and assault the works on that side without waiting for the arrival of the Second Division.

I [James H. Wilson] reached the head of Winslow's Brigade of the Fourth Division at four o'clock, and found the troops marching to the position assigned to them by Gen. Upton. Through an accident, Winslow did not arrive at his position till after dark, but Gen. Upton prepared to make the assault in the night, and coinciding with him in judgment, I ordered the attack.

Three hundred men of the Third Iowa Cavalry, Col. Noble commanding, were dismounted, and, after a slight skirmish, moved forward and formed across the road, under a heavy fire of artillery. The Fourth Iowa and Tenth Missouri were held in readiness to support the assaulting party. At eight and a half o'clock P.M., just as the troops were ready, the enemy at a short distance opened a heavy fire of musketry, and with a four gun battery began throwing canister and grape. Gens. Upton and Winslow in person directed the movement; the troops dashed forward, opened a withering fire from their Spencers, pushed through a slashing abatis, pressed the Rebel line back to their outworks, supposed at first to be their main line. During all this time the rebel guns threw out a perfect storm of canister and grape, but without avail.

Gen. Upton sent two companies of the Tenth Missouri, Captain Glassen commanding, to follow up the success of the dismounted men and get possession of the bridge. They passed through the inner line of works, and, under cover of darkness, before the Rebels knew it, had reached the bridge leading into Columbus.

As soon as everything could be got up to the position occupied by the dismounted men, Gen. Upton, pressed forward again, swept away all opposition, took possession of the foot and railroad bridges, and stationed guards throughout the city.

Twelve hundred prisoners, fifty-two field guns in position for use against us, large quantities of arms and stores fell into our hands. Our loss was only twenty-five killed and wounded. Col. C.A.L. Lamar of Gen. Cobb's staff, formerly owner of the "Wanderer" (slave-trader) was killed.

The splendid gallantry and steadiness of Gen. Upton, Brevet Brig.-Gen. Winslow, and all the officers and men engaged in the night attack

Part of the remains of the CSS *Jackson*, at the National Civil War Naval Museum at Port Columbus. *Author's collection.*

is worthy of the highest commendation. The Rebel force was over three thousand men. They could not believe they had been dislodged from their strong fortifications by an attack of three hundred men...

Before leaving Columbus, Gen. Winslow destroyed the rebel ram Jackson, nearly ready for sea, mounting six seven-inch guns, burned fifteen locomotives, two hundred and fifty cars, the railroad bridge and foot bridges, one hundred and fifteen thousand bales of cotton, four cotton factories, the navy yard, foundry, armory, sword and pistol factory, accoutrement shops, three paper mills, over a hundred thousand rounds of artillery ammunition, besides immense stores of which no account could be taken. The Rebels abandoned and burned the gunboat Chattahoochee, twelve miles below Columbus.[58]

Brigadier General Edward Francis Winslow, who oversaw the destruction of the manufacturing capability of the city of Columbus, described the destruction of the CSS *Jackson* in his report:

MAJOR: I have the honor to submit the following brief account of the gunboat Jackson destroyed at this point yesterday:

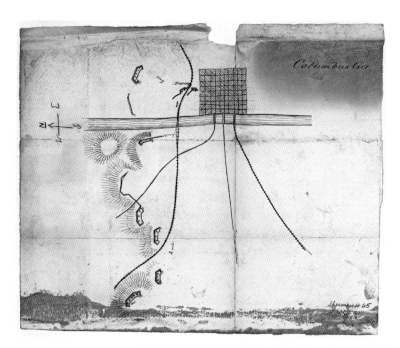

Above: Fortifications near Columbus, Georgia. *Courtesy of the Library of Congress.*

Right: West Point and Columbus fall. *From the* New-York Daily Tribune, *April 26, 1865.*

GEORGIA.

FROM GEN. WILSON'S COMMAND

West Point, Columbus, and Griffin in Our Hands.

CONFIRMATION OF THE FALL OF MACON.

THE REBEL GEN. TYLER KILLED.

GOV. BROWN CALLS OUT THE MILITIA.

The Assassination in Atlanta.

This vessel was intended to be one of the most powerful steamers in the West, and would, if fully completed, have been a formidable antagonist for our river gun-boats or rams. She was about 250 feet in length on deck and about forty feet wide; when fully completed would have drawn from six and a half to seven and a half feet of water; was constructed of live oak; hull two feet thick, with ram of fifteen feet solid oak. The face of the deck was to have been about three and a half feet above water line, but her engines and boilers were below this line. The engines (two) were made here, and were very fine ones; cylinder thirty-six inches and stroke three feet; double connected; four boilers. The armor, which extended just below the water line, was rolled at Atlanta in slabs about six inches wide and two inches thick. These were put on perpendicularly, being curved over the edge of the deck and fastened with bolts two inches in diameter and about two feet apart. The plating was double, breaking joints, and therefore four inches thick. Shot from other vessels could not strike the armor at right angles to its face. The battery consisted of six 7-inch rifled Parrott guns, made at Richmond, Va., and splendidly mounted and finished. They were placed on the main deck, and the gun-room was pyramidal in form, about forty feet long, and twenty feet wide on top. Armor same as on main part of the vessel. There were ten port-holes; the two guns aft and the two forward so arranged that they could be used broadside, making the battery three guns on each side when necessary. This gun-room was about nine feet above deck (from floor to roof), and the pilot-house was raised about two feet above the top of gun-room, heavily plated, sloping sides and ends. The pilot was thus in the gunroom. The engines and boilers were immediately under the guns. There were three hatches, one forward and two aft the gun-room. The boat was to be moved by one screw propeller seven and a half feet in diameter. Lieutenant McLaughlin has been engaged nearly if not quite three years in constructing this vessel, and I am informed she would have been ready for active service in two weeks, or about the 1st of May. The gull-room armor was not in place, but the engines, boilers, and quite a supply of ammunition were on board. When in flames the cables were parted and the gun-boat Muscogee, alias Jackson, floated a way to complete destruction. This description is not scientific, but the result of personal observation, sustained by statements of some mechanics who were employed near the navy-yard. It is of course incomplete, and may be in error in some particulars, but I thought it might be of interest in lack of any better one. A small torpedo-boat went down river the day before the capture of this point.

She is new and in readiness for active duty.

I have the honor to be, your obedient servant,

E.F. WINSLOW,
Brevet Brigadier-General, Commanding Post.[59]

All told, Wilson's Raid was a staggering success. According to the Birmingham Historical Society newsletter, "in 28 days his cavalry corps captured five fortified cities, 288 cannon, and 6,820 prisoners at a cost of 725 Union casualties."[60]

BATTLES FOR MOBILE, ALABAMA

While Mobile Bay had fallen to the Union navy on August 5, 1864, Mobile itself didn't capitulate until April 12, 1865. In order for Mobile to fall, Union forces needed to take the Confederate forts at Spanish Fort and Fort Blakeley.

In March 1865, Major General Edward Canby (head of the Union forces that defeated Henry Sibley in New Mexico in 1862) assembled

"April 1962 SOUTHEAST SCARP—Fort Barrancas, San Carlos & Hovey Roads vicinity, Pensacola, Escambia County, FL." *Courtesy of the Library of Congress.*

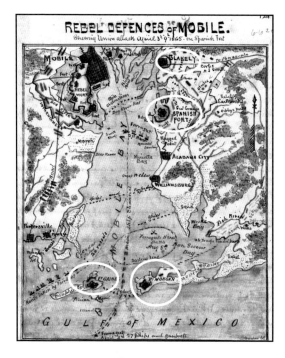

This 1865 map of *Rebel Defenses of Mobile* has Fort Blakeley, Spanish Fort, Fort Morgan and Fort Gaines circled by the author. *Courtesy of the Library of Congress.*

forty-five thousand Union troops at Fort Gaines and Fort Morgan in Alabama and Fort Barrancas in Pensacola, Florida.

On March 16, 1865, Canby led thirty-two thousand of those troops up the eastern side of Mobile Bay, toward Fort Blakeley. On March 19, 1865, Major General Frederick Steele led the rest of the force—about thirteen thousand Union troops—north from Pensacola Bay. Two sieges would quickly ensue:

- March 27, 1865–April 8, 1865: Battle of Spanish Fort, by Canby's forces.

- April 2, 1865–April 9, 1865: Battle of Fort Blakeley (initially attacked by Steele's forces and later joined by part of Canby's force after Spanish Fort fell).

As noted, Fort Blakeley fell on the same day that Lee surrendered to Grant at Appomattox Court House. The next day (April 10, 1865), the evacuation of Mobile began.

Canby in his report discussed the objectives of his move up the east coast of Mobile Bay:

The general plan of operations embraced the reduction of the enemy's works on the east side of Mobile Bay, the opening of the Tensas and Alabama Rivers, reducing the strong works erected for the defense of Mobile, and forcing the surrender or evacuation of the city; or if this was found to involve too great a delay, a direct movement upon Montgomery, shifting for the subsequent

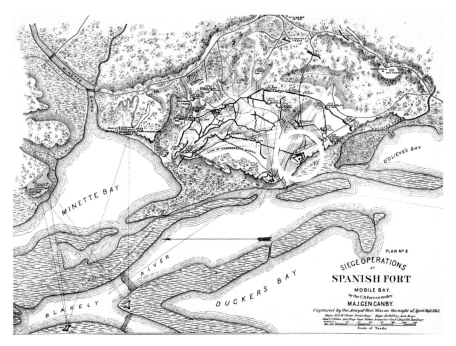

"Siege Operations at Spanish Fort." The Confederate lines are closest to the river. The author has circled Fort McDermott. *Courtesy of the Library of Congress.*

operations of the army the base of supplies from Mobile to Pensacola Bay, and using the railroad from Pensacola to Montgomery for that purpose. In carrying out the first part of this plan the main army, moving by land and water, was to establish itself on firm ground on the east side of Mobile Bay.

Steele, with a sufficient force to meet any opposition that could be sent against him, was to move from Pensacola, threatening Montgomery and Selma, and covering the operations of the cavalry in disabling the railroads. This accomplished, he was to turn to the left and join the main force on Mobile Bay in season for the operations against Spanish Fort and Blakely. Minor operations for the purpose of distracting the enemy's attention were to be undertaken at the same time from Memphis, Vicksburg, Baton Rouge, and the west side of Mobile Bay, and it was expected that Wilson's raid would give full employment to Forrest's rebel cavalry. [Forrest was finally defeated at Selma on April 2, 1865.][61]

The fall of Spanish Fort is discussed in Canby's report. Note the use of field telegraph and the overwhelming amount of artillery arrayed against Spanish Fort:

The time for the bombardment [of Spanish Fort] was anticipated and ordered for 5.30 p.m. of the [April] 8th. At this time there were in position against Spanish Fort fifty-three siege guns (including ten 20-pounder rifles and sixteen mortars) and thirty-seven field pieces. Of these, ten siege rifles and five siege howitzers on our left center enfiladed the enemy's left and center, and five siege howitzers close in on our extreme right enfiladed his center.

The Bay Minette battery against Huger and Tracy consisted of two 100-pounder and four 30-pounder rifles. One of the batteries, No. ___ against Spanish Fort was armed with navy guns and manned by officers and sailors of the squadron, volunteers for this service. The fire of these guns was opened at the appointed time and continued until dark, the troops being in the trenches and prepared to improve any advantage that might be gained. Under cover of the bombardment two companies of the Eighth Iowa, supported by the remainder of the regiment and closely followed by the other regiments of Geddes' brigade, of Carr's division, effected a lodgment on the left of the enemy's line and gained a position from which about 200 yards of his intrenchments could be enfiladed with a musketry fire. This was soon taken, and with it about 200 prisoners, and the captured guns turned upon the enemy.

Night had now fully set in, but Smith was instructed to put his whole force to the work and press it on to completion. A brigade from Veatch's division, then in reserve near Blakely, was ordered by telegraph to report to him, and Granger was advised by telegraph of Smith's progress and instructed to direct the fire and operations on his part so as not to come in conflict with the force at work within the enemy's lines.

This work, led by Colonel Geddes and superintended by Generals Carr and Smith, was pushed on diligently and persistently, and soon after midnight all of the works were in our possession. The brigade from Veatch's division was not needed and was sent back by Smith. The immediate fruits of this success were the capture of these strong forts, two miles of intrenchments with all the armament, material, and supplies, 4 flags, and more than 600 prisoners. The major part of the garrison escaped by the treadway to Fort Tracy, and thence to Blakely and Mobile. In this they were materially aided by the darkness and our imperfect knowledge of the interior of their works. In these last operations the force engaged consisted of one brigade (Bertram's) and one division (Benton's) of the Thirteenth Corps, two divisions (McArthur's and Carr's) of the Sixteenth Corps, with their field batteries; the First Indiana Heavy Artillery, except one company; two companies of the Sixth Michigan Heavy Artillery, and one battery from the navy.[62]

Canby's description of the fall of Fort Blakeley:

From the 6th to the morning of the 9th operations had been steadily carried on against Blakely, meeting with a stubborn resistance from all points of the rebel lines, and particularly on our extreme right, which suffered severely from an enfilading fire from the rebel gun-boats stationed in the mouth of Raft River. With some difficulty in getting up the guns a battery of four 30-pounder rifles was established in a commanding position by the afternoon of the 8th and in a few minutes after opening its fire drove off the gun-boats severely damaged.

Early on the morning of the 9th, and soon after the fall of Spanish Fort was assured, Smith was ordered to move the First and Third Divisions of his corps to the left of the line at Blakely, Garrard's front, and take measures for the assault of that place. Granger was at the same time instructed to leave Bertram's brigade in charge of the captured works and the prisoners and send Benton's division to Steele's front to take part in any operations that might be undertaken. The battery on Bay Minette, No. __, was re-enforced by four 30-pounder Parrotts, and opened fire on Blakely Landing and the

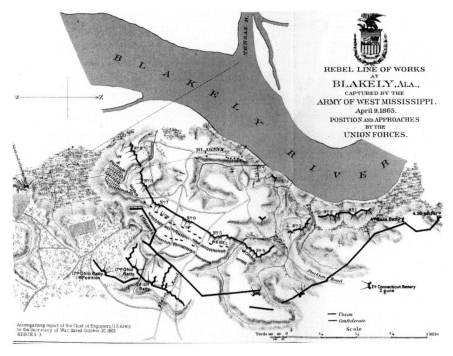

This map of the Battle of Fort Blakeley shows the Union and Confederate (closest to the Blakeley River) lines. *Courtesy of the Library of Congress.*

Tensas River (the water communication between Mobile and Blakely). The fire of the battery, No. __, on our extreme right, was also turned on Blakely Landing, and Mack's battery, six 20-pounder rifles, was put in position on the Pensacola road and opened an effective fire on the rebel batteries.

Orders had also been given to transfer to the Blakely lines as rapidly as possible the siege guns (twenty-eight) and mortars (sixteen) that would be required if the place resisted an assault. In anticipation an additional bridge had been laid down on Bayou Minette, but the impracticable character of the swamp on both sides of the bayou made the approaches to it so difficult that it proved to be of but little service.

In consequence, the divisions of the Thirteenth and Sixteenth Corps did not reach their positions as early as I had anticipated. While waiting their arrival I passed to the right of the line and found that the prospects of a successful assault were promising. The colored division had already gained and held some important advantages on its front and Andrew's and Veatch's divisions were well up with their work, and the resistance of the enemy was less spirited than on previous days. Soon after 4 o'clock Smith had completed his arrangements and telegraphed to me that his two divisions were up and in position.

Garrard had notified Steele that he would be ready to advance at 5.30 p.m., and Benton's division was reported to be crossing the bridge near the left of Steele's front. Steele was then instructed to time his movements with those on the left to advance his line strongly supported, and if possible carry the enemy's works. A little later Benton, who had not yet reached his position, was instructed to turn at once to the left and follow up and support these movements. The line at this time was nearly four miles in length, and the disposition of the troops was as follows: Hawkin's division of colored troops on the right; Andrew's division Thirteenth Corps (two brigades), on the right center; Veatch's division, Thirteenth Corps, on the left center, and Garrard's division, Sixteenth Corps, on the left; one division of the Thirteenth and two of the Sixteenth Corps in support on the right and left. The enemy's line had a development of two miles and a half. It consisted of nine strong redoubts connected by rifle-pits and palisades, and was covered in front by slashings and abatis, and in some places by outworks of telegraph wire and by torpedoes or subterranean shells. The advance was made at the appointed time, and was as nearly simultaneous as it could possibly be from the length of the line and the obstructed character of the ground. With a gallantry to which there were no exceptions the troops pressed forward under a heavy fire of artillery and musketry, passing over exploding torpedoes, net-works, and abatis, and assaulted and carried the enemy's works in about twenty minutes, each

"Storming of Fort Blakely—April 9, 1865." *From the* Harper's Weekly, *April 9, 1865.*

division carrying the works in its front. The immediate results of this victory were flags, all the armament, material, and supplies, and 3,700 prisoners, of whom 3 were generals and 197 commissioned officers of lower grades.[63]

Lieutenant General Richard Taylor, head of Confederate forces in the area, summed up the engagements at Spanish Fort and Fort Blakeley in his memoirs:

On the 26th of March Canby invested Spanish Fort, and began the siege by regular approaches, a part of his army investing Blakeley on the same day. General R.L. Gibson, now a member of Congress from Louisiana, held Spanish Fort with twenty-five hundred men. Fighting all day and working all night, Gibson successfully resisted the efforts of the immense force against him until the evening of April 8th, when the enemy effected a lodgment threatening his only route of evacuation. Under instructions from Maury, he withdrew his garrison in the night to Mobile, excepting his pickets, necessarily left. Gibson's stubborn defence and skilful retreat make this one of the best achievements of the war. Although invested on the 26th of March, the siege of Blakeley was not pressed until April 1st, when Steele's corps of Canby's army joined the original force before it. Here, with a garrison of twenty-eight hundred men, commanded [by] General Liddel, with General Cockrell, now a senator from Missouri, as his second. Every assault of the enemy, who made but little progress, was gallantly repulsed until the afternoon of the 9th, when, learning by the evacuation of Spanish Fort how small a force had delayed him, he concentrated on Blakeley and carried it, capturing the garrison.[64]

On April 12, 1865, Mayor R.H. Slough surrendered the city of Mobile. On April 29, 1865, Edward Canby and Richard Taylor negotiated a

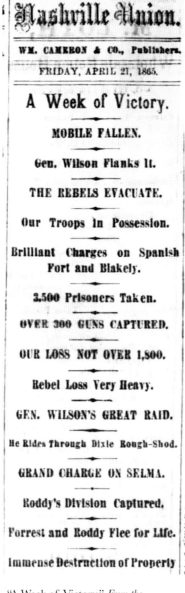

Nashville Union.

WM. CAMERON & CO., Publishers.

FRIDAY, APRIL 21, 1865.

A Week of Victory.

MOBILE FALLEN.

Gen. Wilson Flanks It.

THE REBELS EVACUATE.

Our Troops in Possession.

Brilliant Charges on Spanish Fort and Blakely.

3,500 Prisoners Taken.

OVER 300 GUNS CAPTURED.

OUR LOSS NOT OVER 1,800.

Rebel Loss Very Heavy.

GEN. WILSON'S GREAT RAID.

He Rides Through Dixie Rough-Shod.

GRAND CHARGE ON SELMA.

Roddy's Division Captured.

Forrest and Roddy Flee for Life.

Immense Destruction of Property

"A Week of Victory." *From the* Nashville Union, *April 21, 1865.*

ceasefire at the Magee farm, north of Mobile. Taylor described the surrender in his memoirs:

Intelligence of the Johnston-Sherman convention reached us, and Canby and I were requested by the officers making it to conform to its terms until the civil authorities acted. A meeting was arranged to take place a few miles north of Mobile, where the appearance of the two parties contrasted the fortunes of our respective causes. Canby, who preceded me at the appointed spot, a house near the railway, was escorted by a brigade with a military band, and accompanied by many officers in "full fig." With one officer, Colonel William Levy, since a member of Congress from Louisiana, I made my appearance…. General Canby met me with much urbanity. We retired to a room, and in a few moments agreed upon a truce, terminable after forty-eight hours' notice by either party. Then, rejoining the throng of officers, introductions and many pleasant civilities passed. I was happy to recognize Commodore (afterward Admiral) James Palmer, an old friend. He was second to Admiral Thatcher, commanding United States squadron in Mobile Bay, and had come to meet me. A bountiful luncheon was spread, of which we partook, with joyous poppings of champagne-corks for accompaniment, the first agreeable explosive sounds I had heard for years. The air of "Hail Columbia," which the band in attendance struck up, was instantly changed by Canby's order to that of "Dixie," but I insisted on the first, and expressed a hope that Columbia would be again a happy land, a sentiment honoured by many libations.[65]

Finally, Taylor surrendered his force of forty-seven thousand to Canby:

The party separated [after the ceasefire], *Canby for Mobile, I for Meridian, where within two days came news of Johnston's surrender in North Carolina* [April 26, 1865], *the capture of President Davis in Georgia* [May 10, 1865], *and notice from Canby that the truce must terminate, as his Government disavowed the Johnston-Sherman convention. I informed General Canby that I desired to meet him for the purpose of negotiating a surrender of my forces, and that Commodore Farrand would accompany me to meet Admiral Thatcher. The military and civil authorities of the Confederacy had fallen, and I was called to administer on the ruins as residuary legatee. It seemed absurd for the few there present to continue the struggle against a million of men. We could only secure honourable interment for the remains of our cause—a cause that for four years had fixed the attention of the world, been baptised in the blood of thousands, and whose loss would be mourned in bitter tears by countless widows and orphans throughout their lives. At the time, no doubts as to the propriety of my course entered my mind, but such have since crept in. Many Southern warriors, from the hustings and in print, have declared that they were anxious to die in the last ditch, and by implication were restrained from so doing by the readiness of their generals to surrender. One is not permitted to question the sincerity of these declarations, which have received the approval of public opinion by the elevation of the heroes uttering them to such offices as the people of the South have to bestow; and popular opinion in our land is a court from whose decisions there is no appeal on this side of the grave. On the 8th of May 1865, at Citronelle, forty miles north of Mobile, I delivered the epilogue of the great drama in which I had played a humble part. The terms of surrender demanded and granted were consistent with the honour of our arms; and it is due to the memory of General Canby to add that he was ready with suggestions to soothe our military pride. Officers retained their side-arms, mounted men their horses, which in our service were private property; and public stores, ordnance, commissary, and quartermaster, were to be turned over to officers of the proper departments and receipted for. Paroles of the men were to be signed by their officers on rolls made out for the purpose, and I was to retain control of railways and river-steamers to transport the troops as nearly as possible to their homes and feed them on the road, in order to spare the destitute people of the country the burden of their maintenance. Railways and steamers, though used by the Confederate authorities, were private property, and had been taken by force which the owners could not resist; and it was agreed that they should not be seized by civil jackals following the army without special orders from Washington.*

Finally, I was to notify Canby when to send his officers to my camp to receive paroles and stores.[66]

The war in Alabama was over.

Date	Event(s)
August 5, 1864	Battle of Mobile Bay.
March 1865	Major General Edward Canby assembles forty-five thousand Union troops at Fort Gaines, Fort Morgan and Fort Barrancas (Florida).
March 16, 1865	Canby leads thirty-two thousand troops up the eastern side of Mobile Bay, toward Fort Blakeley.
March 19, 1865	Major General Frederick Steele leads about thirteen thousand Union troops north from Pensacola Bay.
March 27, 1865–April 8, 1865	Battle of Spanish Fort (siege begins on March 27, 1865), by Canby's forces.
April 2, 1865–April 9, 1865	Battle of Fort Blakeley (attack from Steele's forces, later joined by part of Canby's force after Spanish Fort fell).
April 10, 1865	Evacuation of Mobile begins.
April 12, 1865	Mayor R.H. Slough surrenders the city of Mobile.
April 29, 1865	Ceasefire agreement between General Richard Taylor and Union major general Edward Canby at Magee farm, north of Mobile.
May 8, 1865	Forces under General Richard Taylor surrender in Citronelle, Alabama, to Major General Edward Canby.
1981	Alabama legislature names Fort Blakeley a state park.
2011	State funding for Fort Blakeley is suspended; the park now operates on private funds.

Chapter 5

Manufacturing

Josiah Gorgas, working sometimes with private entrepreneurs and sometimes assuming governmental control over facilities, built an iron and armaments industry out of practically nothing in Alabama between 1861 and 1864. The following quote from his diary refers to his tenure as head of the Confederate Ordnance Bureau overall, but it is also true specifically for his actions in Alabama:

> *Where three years ago we were not making a gun, a pistol nor a sabre, no shot nor shell (except at the Tredegar Works)—a pound of powder—we now make all these in quantities to meet the demands of our large armies. In looking over all this I feel that my three years of labor have not been passed in vain.*[67]

Iron ore was mined at Shelby, Tannehill, Bibb, Janney and Cornwall Furnaces, as well as at other sites. Carbines were manufactured at Tallassee. Naval ordnance, gunpowder, ironclads, shovels and horseshoes were manufactured at Selma and iron plating at Shelby. Iron plating, pistols, bayonets and sabers were manufactured across the Chattahoochee River in Columbus, Georgia. Central Alabama had turned into a giant industrial machine by the end of the war.

BRIERFIELD (BIBB) IRONWORKS HISTORICAL STATE PARK

> [A]*rrived at Montevallo* [March 31, 1865]. *Uptons division, having reached there the evening before, destroyed Red Mountain Iron-Works,*

Cahawba Valley Mills, Bibb Iron-Works, Columbiana Works, and much valuable property.[68]

—*Report of Brevet Major General James H. Wilson*

In 1862, the Bibb County Iron Company, led by Caswell Campbell Huckabee, erected a blast furnace in Bibb County. In the earliest days, it mostly produced iron for local users—plows and such. Soon, though, the Confederate government stepped in and put up $20,000 in Confederate bonds to secure one thousand tons of pig iron per year, as well as the construction of a rolling mill.

On September 9, 1863, the Bibb County Iron Company was sold to the Confederate government for $600,000. The Confederate government expanded the mill and completed the rolling mill.

During 1864, pig iron was produced for the Selma Ordnance and Naval Foundry. One hundred Brooke guns were produced with Bibb iron. At its peak, the Bibb Naval Furnace (so named after the Confederate government took over) produced twenty-five tons daily.

On March 31, 1865, the 10th Missouri Cavalry, commanded by Colonel Fredrick Bentee, destroyed the Bibb works.

After the war, a group led by former Confederate ordnance chief Josiah Gorgas bought the Bibb County Iron Company for $45,000 and renamed

Brierfield Furnace as it looks today. *Author's collection.*

Brierfield Furnace, circa 1905.

it Brierfield Coal and Iron Company. Gorgas operated the furnace for three years, but he never really made a go of it. After being sold and leased several times, Brierfield closed forever on Christmas Eve 1894.

Following is the diary entry for October 15, 1865, when Josiah Gorgas visited the site, contemplating its purchase:

> *Sunday,* [October 15] *left after breakfast and rode back by Montevallo to the Bibb Works, 6 miles S. of Montevallo. Here are rolling mills, on the Mahan Creek, & two stacks 2.5 miles west of the Mills. The Rd from Montevallo to Selma passes thro the rolling mills (Briarfield—so named by Lt. Col. Hunt, C.S.A.). A good train connects the mills to the furnaces. There are two good stacks 10ft 4in & 11ft. boshes,*[69] *the latter arranged for hot blast. There are 4000 acres of land. The ore is scattered & not very abundant but sufficient.*

Today, Brierfield is an Alabama State Historical Park.

Date	Event(s)
1862	Bibb County Iron Company, led by Caswell Campbell Huckabee, erects a blast furnace in Bibb County.
	Confederate government advances $20,000 in Confederate bonds to secure one thousand tons of pig iron per year, as well as the construction of a rolling mill.
September 9, 1863	Bibb County Iron Company is sold to the Confederate government for $600,000. The Confederate government expands the mill and completes the rolling mill.
1864	Iron is produced for the Selma Ordnance and Naval Foundry. One hundred Brooke guns are produced with Bibb iron.
March 31, 1865	10th Missouri Cavalry, commanded by Colonel Fredrick Bentee, destroys the Bibb works.
1866	Canebrake Company (under Josiah Gorgas) buys the Bibb County Iron Company for $45,000 and renames it Brierfield Coal and Iron Company.
November 3, 1866	First casting.
July 18, 1867	Blowout at the furnace.
August 1869	Property leased to Thomas Alvis of Virginia.
1873	Alvis goes bankrupt in the Financial Panic.
May 1881	Canebrake Company sells the Brierfield Coal and Iron Company to Alexander Sheppard and William and Kearsley Carter.
mid-1882	Furnace is sold to Thomas Jefferson Peter.
1883	Rolling mill is sold to Peter Huckabee, who produces nails.
December 24, 1894	Furnace blows out, and Brierfield (Bibb) closes forever.
1976	Bibb County opens a park on the site.

Columbus Iron Works

Yes, I am aware that Columbus, Georgia, is not in Alabama. I include it in this list of manufacturing facilities because it is right across the Chattahoochee River from Alabama and because it was the last offensive operation of Wilson's Raid.

In 1853, William R. Brown established the Columbus Iron Works just south of the "modern" Dillingham Bridge. The works began manufacturing small cannons in 1861 and expanded to manufacturing mortars, rifled cannons and twelve-pounders under contract to the Confederate government.

In June 1862, the Confederate navy leased the Columbus Iron Works. Chief engineer James H. Warner began manufacturing engines and boilers for steamships, including the *Chattahoochee* and the *Muscogee* (aka CSS *Jackson*).

On April 16, 1865, in a daring nighttime attack, forces under Major General James Wilson took Columbus, Georgia. The next day, April 17, 1865, Wilson's men destroyed the manufacturing facilities of Columbus, Georgia. The list of facilities destroyed (from General Winslow's report in the *Official Records*) gives some idea of the scope of the manufacturing and textile industries in Columbus during the war:

Having been assigned to the command of this city, I have the honor to make the following report of property captured and destroyed, in obedience to orders from the brevet major-general commanding corps:

Fountain Warehouse: *Six thousand bales C.S.A. cotton.*

Alabama Warehouse: *Seven thousand bales C.S.A. cotton, 100 boxes of tobacco, 20 hogsheads and 100 barrels sugar, and other commissary stores.*

Near Macon Railroad depot: *Three large warehouses containing 20,000 sacks of corn, an immense amount of quartermasters property, commissary stores, and valuable machinery, all in readiness for shipment. A large number of caissons and limbers, generally unserviceable; 100 bales of cotton also 13 locomotives, 10 passenger, 45 box, 24 flat, and 9 coal cars; 1 round-house and machine-shop.*

Naval Armory: *One small rolling-mill in operation; engine, 40-horsepower; 1 blast engine, 8-horsepower; 2 sets of rollers, and 3 furnaces, capable of making 4,000 pounds of iron per day. One new rolling-mill nearly completed;*

one 150-horsepower engine, intended to roll railroad and boiler-plate iron; 3 large furnaces; 1 blast engine, 10-horse-power; one 10-horsepower steam-hammer. This building was 150 feet square. One machine-shop, 2 engines, 45-inch cylinder, nearly completed; 160 feet shafting; 3 small and 2 large planers; 16 iron lathes; 1 large lathe; 7 feet face plate; 3 drill-presses; 30 vises; 15,000 pounds brass. All lathes and planers had full sets of tools. One blacksmith shop, containing 10 forges. Several offices and drawing-rooms, with their contents. One pattern-shop, with 3 wood turning lathes and 1 wood-planer. Foundry, boiler-shop, copper-shop, and their contents.

Navy-Yard: *Containing brass foundry, boat-building house, and 1 machine-shop, with hot-air furnace; 1 engine, 8-horsepower; 1 large planer; 1 rip-saw and drill-press; 5,000 rounds of large ammunition; also 1 blacksmith shop and tools.*

McElhaney & Porters foundry: *Containing 1 engine, 20-horse-power.*

Niter-Works: *Two hundred hands were here employed.*

Muscogee Iron-Works: *Consisting of foundry, machine-shop, small-arms manufactory, blacksmith shop (30 forges), a large saddlers shop, with tools, and 100 sets of flasks; one engine, 30-horsepower.*

C.S. Arsenal: *Consisting of machine-shops, foundries, with two 30-horsepower engines, 2 furnaces, a large amount of machinery and war material; blacksmith shop (16 forges).*

Two powder magazines: *Thirteen thousand pounds of powder, 4,000 loaded shells, 81,000 rounds ammunition for small-arms, and large quantities of rockets, fuses, &c.*

Eagle Oilcloth Factory: *Four-story brick, 150 feet by 50 feet; 136 looms, 3,450 spindles, cotton, and 11,200 spindles, wool; 2,200 yards of jeans, and 1,500 yards osnaburgs made each day.*

Howard Oilcloth Factory: *Five-story brick building with basement, 120 feet by 50 feet; 146 looms, 5,200 spindles, cotton. This factory made 5,000 yards cloth per day.*

Grant Oilcloth Factory: *Three stories and basement, brick building, 70 feet by 40 feet; 60 looms and 2,000 spindles, cotton. Made 2,000 yards cloth each day.*

Haimans Iron Foundry: *One small engine.*

Rock Island Paper Mill: *Manufactured printing, letter, and wrapping paper.*

Columbus Iron-Works: *Sabers, bayonets, and trace-chains were here made; 1,000 stand of arms found.*

Haimans Pistol Factory: *This establishment repaired small-arms, made locks, and was about ready to commence making revolvers similar to Colt army.*

Hughes, Daniel & Co.s Warehouse: *Ten thousand bales of cotton. Presses and type of following-named newspapers: Columbus Sun, Columbus Enquirer, Columbus Times, and the type, one press, &c., of Memphis Appeal.*[70]

One Arsenal Place, Columbus, Georgia. *Author's collection.*

Part of the old Columbus Iron Works still exist. The old drop-forge shop is part of Columbus State University, and the works south of there is now part of the Columbus Visitors' Center. Regarding the old drop-forge shop:

One Arsenal Place occupies the old Drop-Forge shop and warehouse of the Columbus Iron Works. The foundry served as an arsenal of the Confederacy, producing ammunition, mortar and rifled cannon, boilers. Steam engines, and armor plate were manufactured beginning in 1862, when the complex was designated as the Confederate States Naval Iron Works.

Date	Event(s)
1828	Mill city Columbus is created by the Georgia legislature.
1840s	William R. Brown operates a foundry just south of the "modern" Dillingham Bridge.
1853	William R. Brown establishes the Columbus Iron Works. Frederick Law Olmsted states that Columbus is the largest manufacturing city south of Richmond, Virginia.
1860	Columbus textile production is second in the South. Population of Columbus: 9,621; 955 are industrial workers.
1861	Columbus Iron Works begins manufacturing small cannons.
1862	Columbus Iron Works manufacturing mortars, rifled cannons and twelve-pounders under contract to the Confederate government.
June 1862	Confederate navy leases the Columbus Iron Works. Chief Engineer James H. Warner begins manufacturing engines and boilers for steamships, including the *Chattahoochee* and the *Muscogee* (aka CSS *Jackson*).
April 16, 1865	Forces under Major General James Wilson take Columbus, Georgia, at night.
April 17, 1865	Wilson's men destroy the manufacturing facilities of Columbus, Georgia.
August 1866	Columbus Iron Works is back in business.

Date	Event(s)
1872	Columbus Iron Works begins manufacturing ice machines.
1877	Southern Plow Company is created as a subsidiary of the Columbus Iron Works.
1880	Columbus leads the South in textile production.
1880s	Columbus Iron Works ice machines are the best selling in the country (H.D. Stratton models).
April 11, 1902	Fire sweeps through the Columbus Iron Works, except for the foundry.
1902	Teague family of Montgomery takes over as owners.
1925	W.C. Bradley Company purchase the Columbus Iron Works and begins manufacturing stoves and heaters.
1953	First barbecue grills are produced. Bradley Company purchases the ironworks.
1969	Columbus Iron Works is listed in the National Register of Historic Places.
1971	Columbus Iron Works moves out of One Arsenal Place.
1975	The City of Columbus decides to convert part of the Columbus Iron Works into a new visitors' center.
1978	Columbus Iron Works is declared a National Historic Landmark.
1980	Columbus Historic Riverfront Industrial District is declared a National Historic Landmark.

CORNWALL FURNACE PARK, CEDAR BLUFF

In 1855, the Noble Brothers & Company foundry opened in Rome, Georgia. In 1861, it began producing items for the Confederate war effort.

On August 13, 1862, the Confederate government advanced $20,000 for the building of two additional furnaces. Construction of the two new furnaces on the Chattooga River in Cherokee County Alabama began by the end of 1862. The furnaces could produce six tons of ore daily. The furnaces were named Cornwall, after the town that James Noble Sr. came from in England.

In 1864, Sherman twice ordered the destruction of Cornwall Furnace during the Atlanta Campaign.

In 1867, Cornwall Furnace was back in operation. However, the site was not fated for long-term success. In 1870, a furnace stack collapsed after a pile of charcoal caught fire. Production ceased forever after a furnace blow-out in 1874.

On April 24, 1977, Cornwall Furnace Park was officially opened.

Date	Event(s)
1855	Noble Brothers & Company foundry opens in Rome, Georgia.
1861	Noble Brothers & Company begins producing items for the Confederate war effort.
August 13, 1862	Confederate government advances $20,000 for the building of two additional furnaces.

Cornwall Furnace as it appeared in 2015. *Author's collection.*

Date	Event(s)
late 1862	Construction of the two new furnaces on the Chattooga River in Cherokee County, Alabama. The furnaces are named Cornwall, after the town that James Noble Sr. came from in England.
fall 1864	Sherman twice orders the destruction of Cornwall furnace during the Atlanta Campaign.
1867	Furnace is back in operation.
1870	Furnace stack collapses after a pile of charcoal catches fire.
1874	Production ceases forever after a furnace blow-out.
September 27, 1972	Cornwall Furnace is placed in the National Register of Historic Places.
September 25, 1975	Cherokee County Commission purchases the site.
April 24, 1977	Cornwall Furnace Park officially opens.

Irondale Furnace

In the spring of 1863, Wallace S. McElwain began construction on a furnace along Shades Creek in Jefferson County. The furnace was built under contract to the Confederate government to provide iron to the Selma Arsenal. At its peak, the furnace complex comprised 2,146 acres.

It was destroyed on March 29, 1865, by the 4th Iowa during Wilson's Raid. It was back in production in 1866, the first furnace in Alabama to reopen after the Civil War.

It is about a 0.3-mile hike to get to the furnace ruins.

Date	Event(s)
1859	Jones-McElwain and Company Iron Foundry is established at Holly Springs, Mississippi, producing "iron railings, plantation iron, ornamental iron for the fronts of stores and homes, as well as fences and railroad forgings."[71]

Remains of Irondale Furnace. *Author's collection.*

Irondale at its peak.

Date	Event(s)
November 13, 1862	Federal forces occupy Holly Springs.
spring 1863	Wallace S. McElwain begins construction on a furnace along Shades Creek in Jefferson County, Alabama.
spring 1864	Tests for coke (rather than charcoal) use at the furnace.
March 29, 1865	Furnace is destroyed by the 4th Iowa during Wilson's Raid.
1866	Irondale is back in production.
1873	Irondale shuts down for good.
2006	Furnace foundation renovated.

Janney Furnace, Ohatchee

In mid-1863, Alfred A. Janney (pronounced "jane-ee") of Montgomery Alabama, noticed iron ore on a ridge near Ohatchee, Alabama. He and his partner Ned Lewis purchased the property from a local farmer and began construction of Janney Furnace, using slave stonemasons.

Remains of Janney Furnace. *Author's collection.*

Above: Confederate Memorial at Janney Furnace. *Author's collection.*

On July 14, 1864, Union major general Lovell H. Rousseau and a cavalry force of 2,300 men crossed the Coosa River after defeating a Confederate force under Brigadier General James H. Clanton. Rousseau learned of the existence of the new furnace and sent his engineer, Captain Ed Ruger, with a force to destroy the furnace. Ruger and his force destroyed the wooden outbuildings and blew up the furnace, which had probably never been fired.

SELMA ORDNANCE AND NAVAL FOUNDRY

The massive complex of foundries, manufacturing facilities, armories and arsenals in Selma, Alabama, was among the largest of the Civil War in the South. Operations started in 1861, when Colin J. McRae of Mississippi entered into a contract with the Confederate government to make cannons at a factory in Selma.

But the importance of Selma mushroomed when, after the fall of New Orleans in 1862, General Josiah Gorgas, chief of the Confederate Bureau of Ordnance, moved the Mount Vernon Arsenal from near Mobile to Selma.

In 1863, McRae sold the foundry to the Confederate government (for $450,000). Commander Catesby ap Roger Jones (onetime commander of the CSS *Virginia*, aka *Merrimack*) took over running the works to produce naval cannons for ships and coastal defense, including the Brooke gun. The first seven-inch Brooke rifle was cast in July 1863. In time, seventy Brooke guns would be produced at Selma. By 1863–64, there were ten thousand workers and one hundred buildings. Among the largest suppliers of iron to the Selma works were the furnaces in Bibb County, Tannehill Ironworks, Shelby Iron Works and Little Cahaba Iron Works.

Several ironclads were produced here, including the CSS *Tennessee*, CSS *Huntsville* and the CSS *Tuscaloosa*. CSS *Tennessee* would go on to fame and glory under the command of Admiral Franklin Buchanan during the Battle of Mobile Bay.

Selma fell to Union forces under Major General James Wilson on April 2, 1865. The next day, the destruction of the manufacturing base of the city began. The following list of facilities destroyed by the Union cavalry gives some idea of the vastness of the various manufacturing works in Selma (formatting added):

Selma Arsenal, *consisting of twenty-four buildings, containing an immense amount of war material and machinery for manufacturing the same. Very little of the machinery had been removed, although much of it*

Brooke rifle at Fort Morgan, manufactured in Selma, Alabama. *Author's collection.*

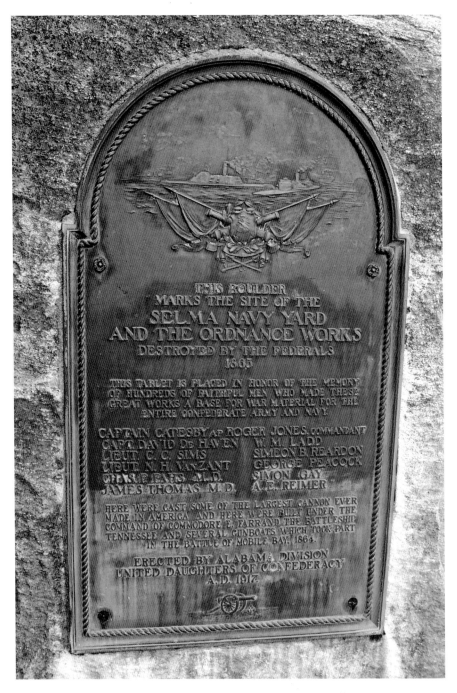

This marker, located at the Old Depot Museum, marks the location of the Selma Ordnance and Naval Foundry. *Author's collection.*

This abandoned building (from a late nineteenth-century factory complex) marks the site of the foundry of the Selma Works. *Author's collection.*

was packed and ready for shipment to Macon and Columbus, Ga. Among other articles here destroyed were 15 siege guns and 10 heavy carriages, 10 field pieces with 60 field carriages, 10 caissons, 60,000 rounds of artillery ammunition, 1,000,000 rounds of small-arm ammunition, 3,000,000 feet of lumber, 10,000 bushels coal, 300 barrels resin, and 3 large engines and boilers.

Second. **Government Naval Foundry**, *consisting of 5 large buildings, containing 3 fine engines, 13 boilers, 29 siege guns unfinished, and all the machinery necessary to manufacture on a large scale naval and siege guns.*

Third. **Selma Iron-Works**, *consisting of 5 buildings, with 5 large engines and furnaces and complete machinery.*

Fourth. **Pierces Foundries**, *Nos. 1 and 2; each of these contained 1 engine, extensive machinery, and a large lot of tools.*

Fifth. **Niter Works***; these works consisted of 18 buildings, 5 furnaces, 16 leaches, and 90 banks.*

Sixth. **Powder mills and magazine***, consisting of 7 buildings, 6,000 rounds of artillery ammunition, and 70,000 rounds of small-arm ammunition, together with 14000 pounds of powder.*

Seventh. **Washington Works***; small iron works with 1 engine.*

Eighth. **Tennessee Iron-Works***, containing engines.*

Ninth. **Phelan and McBrides machine-shop***, with 2 engines.*

Tenth. **Horseshoe manufactory***, containing 1 engine. About 8,000 pounds of horseshoes from this establishment were used by our army.*

Eleventh. **Selma Shovel Factory***; this factory contained 1 steam engine, 8 forges, and complete machinery for manufacturing shovels, railroad spikes, and iron axle-trees for army wagons.*

Twelfth. On the **Alabama and Mississippi Railroad***, 1 round-house, 1 stationary engine, and much standing machinery, together with 20 box and 2 passenger cars.*

Thirteenth. On the **Tennessee Railroad***, 1 round-house, with machinery, 5 locomotives, 1 machine, 19 box and 50 platform cars.*

Fourteenth. **In the fortifications***, one 30-pounder Parrott gun, four 10-pound guns, 11 field pieces, 10 caissons, 2 forges, and 500 rounds of fixed ammunition. A portion of the guns destroyed in the arsenal were those captured on the fortifications at the time of the assault. The machinery, engines, and the trunnions of the guns were broken before being burned. The arsenal buildings were of wood with but few exceptions. The foundry buildings were of brick. Together with all other buildings enumerated, these were completely destroyed without firing other than public buildings. Several buildings were fired on the evening of the 2d instant, and quite a number of private dwellings were thereby consumed. This burning being done without authority destroyed supplies which would have been useful to the army, and did no particular damage to the enemy. I cannot estimate in dollars the value* *of the public property destroyed, but all can readily see that the value in a mechanical, social, and war point of view is almost inestimable.*

Respectfully submitted.
E.F. WINSLOW,

Brevet Brigadier-General, Commanding Post.[72]

The current circa 1890 L&N depot (now a museum) is built on the site of the old foundry and has a monument on the property noting the onetime existence of the Selma Ordnance and Naval Foundry.

Date	Event(s)
1861	Colin J. McRae of Mississippi enters into a contract with the Confederate government to make cannons at a factory in Selma.
1862	After the fall of New Orleans in 1862, General Josiah Gorgas, chief of the Confederate Bureau of Ordnance, moves the Mount Vernon Arsenal from near Mobile to Selma.
1863	McRae sells the foundry to the Confederate government (for $450,000); Commander Catesby ap Roger Jones takes over running the Works to produce naval cannons for ships and coastal defense, including the Brooke gun.
July 1863	First seven-inch Brooke rifle cast.
1863–64	Ten thousand workers and one hundred buildings. CSS *Tennessee* built.
December 1864	Last Brooke gun is cast (some sources say March 21, 1865).
April 3, 1865	Selma Ordnance and Naval Foundry is destroyed after Major General James Wilson takes the city.
circa 1890	The current L&N depot (now a museum) is built on the site of the old foundry.

SHELBY IRON WORKS

Shelby Iron Works was founded in the 1840s by Horace Ware. In 1852, it began supplying iron ore to an iron foundry in Columbus, Georgia. In April 1860, on the eve of the Civil War, it added a rolling mill to manufacture iron plate. During the war, several ironclads were manufactured using Shelby plate, including the CSS *Tennessee* (of Mobile Bay fame) and the CSS *Mobile*.

On April 21, 1862, Shelby Iron Works signed a contract with the Confederate government to deliver twelve thousand tons of ore each year. Most of the ore went to the naval works in Selma.

In the spring of 1863, all mining activities were put under the control of the Nitre and Mining Bureau. Operations of the Shelby works were controlled by the central government until the end of the war. As an example

Above: Remains of the Shelby Iron Furnace. *Author's collection.*

Left: Shelby Iron. *From the Nashville Union and American, September 30, 1870.*

of the government control in action, in October 1863, the company tried to build a railroad spur to nearby Columbiana, but the Nitre and Mining Bureau stepped in to stop the construction.

By the end of 1864, life was becoming more difficult for the Shelby Works. Production slowed because of food shortages. Clothing shortages lead to an outbreak of pneumonia in the mines.

On March 31, 1865, the rolling mill, blast engine and boiler machinery were destroyed by troops under General Emory Upton (during Wilson's Raid).

Unlike some of the other iron mines and works destroyed by Wilson's Raid, Shelby was back up and running by 1869, when a furnace was put into blast. By 1870, Shelby was manufacturing railroad wheels, and in 1872, Furnace No. 2 opened.

Josiah Gorgas discussed the state of the Shelby Works after the war in his diary entry of October 14, 1865:

> *Saturday* [October 14] *reached Shelby Iron Works about noon, & stopped at Mr. Hall's. This property is five miles from Columbia & has track laid to it. It has very good ore beds very convenient. There is one fire stack—11 feet bosh* [the lower portion of a blast furnace]*—& another smaller partly finished. There is also a rolling mill. The improvements are very good. The country is pleasant, & altogether the establishment is very attractive. They will have to bring coal & coke a distance of about 30 to 35 miles by rail. The destruction by the enemy did a great deal of damage to the works. The company, however, is preparing to go on.*[73]

In 1923, Shelby Iron Works closed for good. Although many of the ironworks buildings were dismantled for scrap in 1929, there's still a fair number of buildings standing from the Shelby Works, including a chemical plant, a post office, an 1870s sawmill and a hotel.

Date	Event(s)
1840s	Horace Ware begins the construction of a cold-blast charcoal iron furnace in Shelby County.
1846–49	Furnace goes into operation.
1852	Shelby Iron Manufacturing Company begins supplying iron ore to an iron foundry in Columbus, Georgia.
1858	Shelby County Iron Manufacturing Corporation is created.

The 1900 Shelby Hotel, located next to the Shelby Iron Works Park on Highway 42. *Author's collection*.

World War I–era Shelby Chemical Company plant. *Author's collection*.

Date	Event(s)
1860	Shelby Furnace town site has three hundred inhabitants.
April 1860	Rolling mill goes into operation (the first of its kind in Alabama).
1862	Ware sells most of his shares; company is renamed Shelby Iron Company. CSS *Tennessee* and *Mobile* constructed with Shelby plating. The ironworks expands as demand for iron rises.
March 1862	Noted Welsh iron master Giles Edwards comes to Shelby to supervise the enlargement of the works.
April 21, 1862	Contract signed with Confederate government to deliver twelve thousand tons of ore each year. Most of the ore goes to the naval works in Selma.
spring 1863	All mining activities are put under control of the Nitre and Mining Bureau.
October 1863	The company completes the road bed for a railroad spur to Columbiana, but the Nitre and Mining Bureau nixes actual construction of the railroad.
winter 1864	Production slows because of food shortages.
December 1864	Clothing shortages lead to an outbreak of pneumonia in the mines.
January 1865	Railroad spur to Columbiana is completed, connecting to the Alabama and Tennessee River Railroad.
March 31, 1865	Rolling mill, blast engine and boiler machinery destroyed by troops under General Emory Upton (during Wilson's Raid). At war's end, Shelby was owed $250,000 from the Confederate government.
1866	Sale of stock to finance reconstruction costs.
1868–70	Three-story brick commissary is built.
1868	School opens.

Date	Event(s)
February 1869	First furnace up and running since Wilson's Raid.
1870	Manufacture of railroad wheels begins.
1872	Company store opens.
1875	Furnace No. 2 opens, with a seventy-five-ton capacity.
1881	Last of Ware's stock is bought out.
1889	A third furnace is added.
1890	Majority position in the stock is sold to a New Jersey Corporation.
August 24, 1890	Alabama Mineral Railroad begins operation of the railroad spur to Columbiana.
1898	Original hotel burns (built 1863).
1900	Hotel is rebuilt on original site (still standing today).
1923	Shelby Iron Works closes for good.
1929	Many ironworks buildings are dismantled for scrap.
1930	Shelby Iron Company becomes the Alabama Corporation.

TALLASSEE

In January 1844, Thomas M. Barnett and William M. Marks built a six-story stone cotton mill on the Tallapoosa River in Tallassee. By 1857, the mill was known as the Tallassee Falls Manufacturing Company. The building would later serve as the heart of the Civil War armory and carbine factory.

In April 1864, as Grant moved inexorably closer to Richmond, Colonel Josiah Gorgas sent Lieutenant Colonel James Burton (superintendent of armories) and Captain C.P. Boles from Richmond to Tallassee to assess whether it was feasible to move the Richmond Carbine Factory from Richmond to the Tallassee Manufacturing Company. They chose the aforementioned 1844 stone cotton mill building as the new home for the armory because of its remoteness.

On June 1, 1864, Captain C.P. Boles was put in charge of renovations and operations at the new Tallassee Armory. That summer, Colonel Josiah Gorgas moved the Richmond Carbine Factory from Richmond to the

Rear of the Tallassee Armory, as seen from Outer Drive. *Author's collection.*

Tallassee Manufacturing Company. By October 1864, the factory had already manufactured one hundred carbines (.58-caliber muzzle-loading carbines, 40.5 inches long).

Tallassee was the only Confederate armory in Alabama that had escaped destruction by the end of the war. In late March 1865, using a poor map, Wilson's forces passed ten miles to the east (Franklin) of the Tallassee Confederate Armory and failed to destroy it.

By April 7, 1865, much of the armory contents had been packed for shipment to Georgia, but after the fall of Columbus on April 16, 1865, the Tallassee Armory ceased operations the next day.

Much of the original armory still exists, as well as three of four houses on King Street that were built for use by Confederate officers.

Date	Event(s)
January 1844	Thomas M. Barnett and William M. Marks build a six-story stone cotton mill on the Tallapoosa River.
1857	Renamed Tallassee Falls Manufacturing Company.

Ruins of the Tallassee Armory from the dam. *Author's collection.*

One of four (three are still extant) Confederate officers' quarters built in 1864. This is the one at 301 King Street. *Author's collection.*

Date	Event(s)
April 1864	Colonel Josiah Gorgas sends Lieutenant Colonel James Burton (superintendent of armories) and Captain C.P. Boles from Richmond to Tallassee to assess whether it was feasible to move the Richmond Carbine Factory from Richmond to the Tallassee Manufacturing Company. They chose the old 1844 stone building for the armory because of its remoteness.
June 1, 1864	Captain C.P. Boles is put in charge of renovations and operations.
summer 1864	Colonel Josiah Gorgas moves Richmond Carbine Factory from Richmond to the Tallassee Manufacturing Company.
October 1864	One hundred carbines have been manufactured.
February 1865	Boles requests and receives a transfer and is replaced by Major W.V. Taylor.
March 1865	Using a poor map. Wilson's force passes ten miles to the east of the Tallassee Confederate Armory and fails to destroy it.
April 7, 1865	Much of the armory contents are packed for shipment to Georgia, as Wilson's forces near Tallassee.
April 17, 1865	Tallassee Armory ceases operations.
2006	Fire at the old armory destroys one of the buildings.

TANNEHILL (ROUPES VALLEY)

During the day Company I and Company D were ordered off to the left of the line to burn a large iron works and smelter [Tannehill]. *I was on the advance of this party and as we rode up to the works there was a large collection of colored ladies in front of a building and one of them addressed me saying, "What are you all guine to do?" I told her we were going to burn the iron works. She replied I am powerful glad of that for it uses up any amount* [of my people] *every year.*[74]
                                —*Sergeant George Monlux, 8ᵗʰ Iowa Cavalry*

Tannehill Furnace. *Author's collection.*

Wilson's cavalry destroyed the great ironworks at Tannehill, west of modern Birmingham, on March 31, 1865. *Author's collection.*

As early as 1830, Daniel Hillman, a Pennsylvania ironworker, built a bloomery forge on the site of Tannehill (Roupes Valley) named Roupes Valley Ironworks. The name Tannehill came into the picture in 1836 when Ninian Tannehill took over operations.

Between 1859 and 1863, three furnaces were constructed using slave labor. Tannehill No. 1 was built by the famous Moses Stroup, who also built Etowah Iron Works in Cartersville, Georgia.

During its heyday during the Civil War, Tannehill was capable of producing twenty-two tons of pig iron per day, most of it going to the Selma Arsenal and Gun Works.

On March 31, 1865, the 8th Iowa Cavalry under Captain William A. Sutherland destroyed the ironworks as part of Wilson's Raid.

In 1868, the mining of brown ore and the production of pig iron was resumed on the site by the Pioneer Mining and Manufacturing Company (Republic Steel Corporation).

In 1969, the Tannehill Ironworks Historical State Park was established. There are a number of nineteenth-century buildings (although most are from 1870 or later) in the park, as well as significant remains of Furnaces No. 1, No. 2 and No. 3.

Date	Event(s)
1830	Daniel Hillman, a Pennsylvania ironworker, builds a bloomery forge on the site, named Roupes Valley Ironworks.
1836	Ninian Tannehill takes over operations (Daniel Hillman died in 1832).
1852	Moses Stroup, builder of the Etowah Ironworks in Cartersville, Georgia, moves to Alabama.
1859–63	Three furnaces are constructed using slave labor—Tannehill No. 1 was built by Moses Stroup.
1862	Moses Stroup joins the Red Mountain Iron & Coal Company and builds the furnace at Oxmoor. William L. Sanders purchases the Tannehill operation.
March 31, 1865	8th Iowa Cavalry under Captain William A. Sutherland destroys the ironworks as part of Wilson's Raid.

Date	Event(s)
1865–67	Small scrap (cupola) furnace is operated at Tannehill by B.J. Jordan and later James T. Loveless.
1868	Mining of brown ore and making pig iron resumes on the site by the Pioneer Mining and Manufacturing Company (Republic Steel Corporation).
1952	The furnaces are donated to the University of Alabama by Republic Steel.
1969	Tannehill Ironworks Historical State Park is established.
1976	Tannehill Furnace No. 1 is refired.
1981	Tannehill Museum opens.

WHAT IS LEFT TO SEE

- Brierfield (Bibb) Ironworks Historical State Park (240 Furnace Parkway, Brierfield, AL, 35035)
- Columbus Iron Works (One Arsenal Place, Front Avenue, Columbus, GA)
- Cornwall Furnace Park (1200 County Road 251, Cedar Bluff, AL, 35959)
- Irondale Furnace (4171 Stone River Road, Mountain Brook, Alabama)
- Janney Furnace (145 Janney Road, Ohatchee, AL, 36271)
- National Civil War Naval Museum at Port Columbus (1002 Victory Drive, Columbus, GA, 31901)
- Selma Ordnance and Naval Foundry marker (4 Martin Luther King Jr. Street, Selma, AL, 36701)
- Shelby Iron Works (10268 Co Road 42, Shelby, AL, 35143)
- Tallassee Armory (1844 Outer Drive, Tallassee, AL, 36078)
- Tannehill Ironworks Historical State Park (12632 Confederate Parkway, McCalla, AL, 35111)

Chapter 6

Prison Camps

CAHABA

The Confederate prison at Cahaba, Alabama (17 First South Street, Orrville, Alabama, 36737) was located at the confluence of the Cahaba and Alabama Rivers. It held prisoners on and off between 1863 and 1865. It was located in an old cotton shed and had bunks for about five hundred men. By October 1864, Cahaba had two thousand prisoners, many of whom had to sleep outside.

Cahaba is located in south-central Alabama and is surrounded by swamps and the aforementioned rivers. One can only imagine what effect the heat and insects had on the men held there in the 1860s.

Other Civil War prisons in Alabama included those in Tuscaloosa and Montgomery. The prison(s) at Tuscaloosa were used in the earliest days of the war to house Union soldiers captured at First Manassas (Bull Run) and shipped to Alabama. Sergeant Henry Wirz was in charge of the prison at Tuscaloosa before he took over as commandant of Andersonville, Georgia.

The Confederate Military Prison at Montgomery is marked by a historic marker on Tallapoosa Street at Coosa Street, Montgomery, Alabama:

[Side 1:] *Near this site, from mid April to December 1862, a Confederate military prison held, under destitute conditions, 700 Union soldiers, most*

This drawing in the Library of Congress Civil War Collection is identified as Cahaba prison, although that identification is disputed (Cahaba had a brick, rather than wooden, fence around it). *Courtesy of the Library of Congress.*

This chimney stands on the location of the old Cahaba prison. It may be the chimney from the old cotton shed, but some dispute this. *Author's collection.*

captured at Shiloh. They were imprisoned in a foul, vermin-abounding cotton depot, 200 feet long and 40 feet wide, without blankets and only the hard earth or wood planks as a bed. The cotton shed was situated between Tallapoosa Street and the Alabama River. Of the 700 Union prisoners, nearly 198 died in captivity. The survivors were moved to Tuscaloosa, Alabama in December 1862.

[Side 2:] *Records of the Commissary General of Prisoners list 198 Union prisoners, from the Montgomery military prison, buried at Montgomery. Most of these were listed as unknown. Subsequently, in 1868, the remains interred in the Montgomery cemetery were removed to the National Cemetery at Marietta, Georgia. Over 674,000 soldiers were taken captive during the Civil War. Often prisoners were crammed into facilities with disregard of capacity limits, hygiene, nutrition, or sanitation needs. These deplorable conditions existed in military prisons of both sides. More than 56,000 prisoners died in confinement, 30,218 in Confederate and 25,976 in Union prisons.*

Chapter 7

Forts

FORT BLAKELEY

The town of Blakeley was founded by Josiah Blakeley in 1813, when he purchased 7,000 acres (later surveys indicated that it was actually 2,280 acres) of land and hired a surveyor to lay out the town.

While Josiah Blakeley died in 1815, the town flourished, reaching a population of more than four thousand in the 1820s. The town was officially incorporated by the new state of Alabama in 1820. Shipbuilding was an important business in Blakeley—the steamers *Mississippi* and *Tensas* were both built there. The town also offered port facilities and, at one time, was actually in competition with Mobile as a port.

The town started to atrophy after yellow fever epidemics in 1822, 1826 and 1828. By the beginning of the Civil War in 1861, there were only one hundred residents left. The population would soon swell, as Confederate forces of up to four thousand were stationed at Fort Blakeley.

The Battle of Fort Blakeley was fought from April 2, 1865, to April 9, 1865. For a description of the battle, see the section "Battles for Mobile, Alabama."

In 1981, Historic Blakeley State Park was formed, which includes the scant ruins of the old town (jail and cemetery), as well as significant ruins from the fort.

Confederate Redoubt No. 4 at Fort Blakeley. *Author's collection.*

Graves of nineteenth-century smallpox victims in Blakeley. *Author's collection.*

Union redoubt at Fort Blakeley. *Author's collection.*

Date	Event(s)
1806	Josiah Blakeley moves from Connecticut to Mobile.
July 1813	Blakeley is founded by Josiah Blakeley, who purchases 2,280 acres of land; Blakeley hires surveyor James Magoffin to lay out the town.
January 6, 1814	The Mississippi territorial legislature authorizes Blakeley as a town.
1815	Josiah Blakeley dies.
December 12, 1818	*Blakeley Sun* newspaper begins publishing.
1819	First steamboat in Alabama built in Blakeley—the *Tensas.*
1820	State of Alabama incorporates Blakeley.
1820–68	Becomes county seat of Baldwin County.
winter 1822	Population: 2,700.
1822, 1826 and 1828	Yellow fever epidemics.

Date	Event(s)
1826–66	Post office in Blakeley.
1861	Population: 100.
1864–65	Confederate forces of up to four thousand are stationed at Fort Blakeley.
April 2, 1865–April 9, 1865	Battle of Fort Blakeley.
1974	The town site is listed in the National Register of Historic Places.
1981	Historic Blakeley State Park is formed.
1993	Blakeley is named a Class A Civil War site by the United States Congress.
2011	State funding is withdrawn.

FORT GAINES

In 1821, construction began on Fort Gaines, but it soon halted as funds dried up. In 1845, Congress allocated $20,000 to continue construction on Fort Gaines, which was officially named in 1853 after War of 1812 hero General Edmund Pendleton Gaines.

In 1857, construction resumed after many years of insufficient funding. The original fort design was completely modified by army chief engineer Joseph Totten.

On January 5, 1861, the Alabama state militia seized the fort, which was soon turned over to the control of the Confederate government. The Confederate government finally completed construction of the fort in 1862.

On August 3, 1864, 1,500 Union troops were stationed west of Fort Gaines, preparing for an assault. By the next day, they were dug in half a mile from the fort; 800 Confederate troops held Fort Gaines.

On August 5, 1864, the Battle of Mobile Bay occurred, with Fort Gaines holding out until August 8, 1864, when it was surrendered by Colonel Charles D. Anderson.

The capture of Fort Gaines was announced by General Edward Canby in a report dated August 9, 1864:

Bastion at Fort Gaines. *Author's collection.*

Modern photo of Fort Gaines. *Author's collection.*

New Orleans, LA., August 9, 1864.
(Received 9.40 a.m. 16th.)

Sir: Fort Gaines, with 46 commissioned officers and 818 enlisted men, with its armament, 26 guns intact, and provisions for twelve months, has surrendered unconditionally. It was occupied by our forces at 8 o'clock yesterday morning. Fort Powell was abandoned, its garrison escaping to Cedar Point; its armament, 18 guns, is in condition for immediate service. General Granger, re-enforced by 2,000 men, will immediately invest Fort Morgan, leaving garrisons in Forts Gaines and Powell.

Ed. R.S. Canby,
Major-General.[75]

A more detailed account of the capture follows, from M.D. McAlester, captain and chief engineer:

Office of Chief Engineer, Military Division of West Mississippi,

New Orleans, August 20, 1864.

General: I have the honor to submit the following brief account of the very brief investment of Fort Gaines by our combined land and naval forces, resulting in its fall:

…We landed on Dauphin Island, seven miles from Fort Gaines, at 4 p.m. on the 3rd of August. On the 4th, at 10 a.m., our line of sentinels being within 1,200 yards of the fort, I established a line of intrenchments and batteries across the island (see sketch herewith), and at 4 p.m. work was commenced. During the night we got up six 3-inch Rodman guns and put them in position in the sand ridge.

On the 5th, at sunrise, the fleet (four monitors and fourteen wooden ships-twelve wooden ships and gun-boats remained outside the bar) started on its way by the forts, and we opened fire upon Fort Gaines with the 3-inch guns. The fort replied warmly but did no damage. Three monitors and the fourteen ships reached the bay in safety. After the entrance of the fleet, and while it was engaged with the ram Tennessee, Fort Gaines opened upon it within two 10-inch columbiads, which bore upon the scene of action. These we shortly silenced by our field guns from the sand-hills, which saw the columbiads (unprotected by parados or traverses) fairly in reserve and flank.

On the 6th the double-turreted monitor *Winnebago, four 11-inch guns,* approached to a half mile of Fort Gaines, and opened fire upon it with very good effect, bursting many shells over it and taking the opposite sides of the fort well in reserve (no parados or traverses). The fort replied with two 10-inch guns, but did not hit the monitor. At night Fort Powell was blown up and abandoned by the enemy.

On the 7th we were nearly ready to open fire with four 30-pounders and the six field guns, and the infantry trench was nearly complete, giving considerable cover.

On the 8th, at 10 a.m., Fort Gaines surrendered to our combined land and naval forces unconditionally. The garrison consisted of 818 officers and men. The armament was four 10-inch columbiads, two 7-inch Brooke rifles, twelve or fifteen smooth-bores (24s and 32d), and five or six flank casemate howitzers. There was an abundant supply of ammunition and rations for two months. Two 10-inch guns and six 24s bore upon the land approach.

I found the fort in excellent order, finished fully up to the plan in possession of our Engineer Department, a copy of which I have, but with its guns lying over the crest of the parapet, without merlons, traverses, or parados for their protection, or splinter-proofs for the protection of the cannoneers. It was utterly weak and inefficient against our attack (land and naval), which would have taken all its fronts in front, enfilade, and reserve. With our guns in the sand ridge we could have placed every shot upon the terre-pleins of the opposite fronts. This sand ridge (indicated on the Coast Survey maps) extends along the southern shore of the island, and affords a perfect cover up to a point about 400 yards from the fort. Its height varies between fifteen and thirty feet, the crest of the fort being in reference (twenty-seven feet). The garrison had commenced four heavy traverses, but had made little progress with them. It is probable we should have dismounted the guns before they could have been covered. The construction of good traverses, merlons, and parados, that shall not take up too much room, is a matter of considerable time and labor, if the material has to be brought from any distance and elevated to high terre-pleins, as was the case at Fort Gaines. It was easy for us to land our guns, take them to the front, put them in battery, and open fire before the defense could get its guns under cover.

I send a map of Dauphin Island herewith, with my line of works laid down. The left is thrown back in consequence of the enemy occupying Little Dauphin Island with artillery.

Anchor from the USS *Hartford*, Admiral Farragut's flagship. *Author's collection.*

Very respectfully, your obedient servant,

M.D. MCALESTER,
Captain and Chief Engineer.
Brigadier General R. DELAFIELD,
Chief Engineer, Washington, D.C.[76]

In 1901–4, six new batteries were added to Fort Gaines. During World War I, the Coastal Artillery was stationed at the fort. During World War II, the fort was used by the Alabama National Guard and the U.S. Coast Guard. In 1955, it became a state park.

Date	Event(s)
1519	Dauphin Island and Mobile Bay are mapped by Alonzo Pineda.
1821	Construction begins on Fort Gaines (although the original design was made in 1818–19). Construction halts when funds dry up.

Date	Event(s)
1845	Congress allocates $20,000 to continue construction on Fort Gaines.
1853	Fort is named for War of 1812 General Edmund Pendleton Gaines.
1857	Construction resumes after many years of insufficient funding. The original fort design is completed modified by U.S. Army chief engineer Joseph Totten.
January 5, 1861	Alabama state militia seizes the fort and soon turns it over to the Confederate government.
1862	Construction on the fort is (finally) completed (by the Confederate government).
August 3, 1864	About 1,500 Union troops are stationed west of Fort Gaines, preparing for an assault. By the next day, they are dug in half a mile from the fort.
August 5, 1864	Battle of Mobile Bay.
August 8, 1864	Fort Gaines is surrendered by Colonel Charles D. Anderson.
1901–4	Six new batteries are added.
World War I	Coastal Artillery is stationed at Fort Gaines.
post–World War I	The fort is sold to the State of Alabama by the U.S. War Department.
World War II	Used by the Alabama National Guard and the U.S. Coast Guard.
1955	Opens as a state park.
December 12, 1976	Listed in the National Register of Historic Places.
March 18, 2009	Listed as "one of the nation's 10 most endangered battle sites" by the Civil War Preservation Trust.
2011	Placed on a list of "Most Endangered Historic Places" by the National Trust for Historic Preservation.

FORT McDERMOTT (SPANISH FORT)

During its life, since about 1712, Spanish Fort has been administered under several different flags, including French, English, American and Confederate States of America. Around 1780, a Spanish fort was built on the site by General Bernardo de Galvez—it is from this fort that the town gets its name.

By the end of the War of 1812, Spanish Fort was in the hands of the United States. Then, in 1861, it was seized by Alabama militia and soon transferred to the Confederate States of America. Fortifications were built there to protect Mobile, just across Mobile Bay.

Fort McDermott (Redoubt No. 2) was part of a two-mile-long line of Confederate fortifications at Spanish Fort. During the Battle of Spanish Fort (March 27–April 8, 1865), Fort McDermott was manned by about two hundred soldiers from Georgia, Louisiana and Arkansas. They defended the redoubt for almost two weeks from incessant Union attacks, but the fort was finally abandoned on April 8, 1865.

For many years, Fort Blakeley was covered with vines and underbrush, until the Sons of Confederate Veterans Raphael Semmes Camp 11 cleared three acres of the fort, which is now open to the public (although it remains a private park). There are several parking spaces at the intersection of Cannonade Boulevard and Spanish Main Street.

Newly cleared Fort McDermott, Spanish Fort, Alabama. *Author's collection.*

Date	Event(s)
1712	Spanish Fort is used as a trading post by the French.
1763	Spanish Fort ceded to the British in the Treaty of Paris.
1780	After the British lose control of Spanish Fort during the Revolutionary War, a Spanish fort is built on the site by General Bernardo de Galvez.
1781	The British launch an unsuccessful attack on Spanish Fort.
1815	As a result of the War of 1812, Spanish Fort is ceded to the United States.
1819	Spanish Fort is now part of the Alabama Territory.
1864	Fort McDermott is established as the high point of a two-mile line of fortifications at Spanish Fort, Alabama.
March 27–April 8, 1865	The Battle of Spanish Fort is a victory for the attacking Union forces.
April 2–April 9, 1865	Battle of Fort Blakeley (Union victory).
July 19, 1993	Modern-day city of Spanish Fort established.
April 11, 2015	Sons of Confederate Veterans Raphael Semmes Camp 11 holds a dedication day for the Fort McDermott Confederate Memorial Park.

FORT MORGAN

The first fort built on this site was Fort Bowyer in 1813. A battle occurred there on September 15, 1814, as part of the War of 1812. The Battle of Fort Bowyer was an American victory against the British and a number of Creek Indians.

In 1819, the U.S. Army Corps of Engineers began construction on Fort Morgan. The masonry was completed in 1834, and the fort was named in honor of Revolutionary War hero General Daniel Morgan.

On January 4, 1861, Fort Morgan was seized by Alabama militia in a lead-in to the Civil War. The Confederate army took control of Fort Morgan in March 1861.

The Battle of Mobile Bay occurred on August 5, 1864, but Fort Morgan didn't fall until almost three weeks later. After a fierce Union bombardment on

The imposing walls of Fort Morgan. *Author's collection*.

Interior of casemates at Fort Morgan. *Author's collection*.

August 22, 1864, Brigadier General Richard L. Page surrendered Fort Morgan the next day, after his magazines were threatened by Union bombardment. In all, 581 men surrendered, while 17 were killed in the bombardment.

The "Bombardment and Capture of Fort Morgan" was recorded in this contemporary newspaper article:

New Orleans, Aug. 24. The heavy bombardment of Fort Morgan which began early on Monday morning, the 22d is perhaps the most severe firing which has yet been directed against the rebel fortifications except Fort Sumpter [sic], the range was obtained previous to the opening of the cannonade on that day, so on the morning of the 22nd Com. Farragut's fleet, including the flag ship and other large vessels, the mortars, the ram Tennessee *and some blockading vessels, took part in the bombardment, in conjunction with the land forces. These were situated on Mobile Point in the rear of the fort, and heavy mortar batteries were planted within. The vessels were stationed on either side of Mobil Point, and the front was therefore invested on three sides. The firing from early dawn until 6 o'clock was regular and effective, but shortly after that hour it became rapid and extremely heavy.*

The sight, from Fort Gaines and other points, from which the joint operations of the fleet and the land force could be witnessed, covered the entire field, and the appearance of the bombardment is described as most grand and stirring. The bursting of the heavy shells in the fort or over it was constant, and for four hours the rebel garrison received in that way an average of about, one shell per minute.

The monitors fired at close range. Their aim was unusually good and the explosion of their 11 and 18-inch shells could be distinguished from the bursting of the shells thrown by the other guns, which were of smaller calibre. The ram Tennessee *assisted in this action and did good service.*

The large vessels of the fleet poured in continuous broadsides, and the rear of the fort was covered by the fire of the army. The regular discharge of cannon in various directions around the fortifications, the flying of the shells and their loud and often simultaneous explosion, cannot be adequately described. This rapid work continued till 10 o'clock and then slackened somewhat, though the firing was kept up. In all this time the rebels, who were driven from their guns, did very little work.

An officer who witnessed the whole of the heavy bombardment was able to distinguish but four shots from Ft. Morgan, after the principle work of the day began from our batteries. It does not appear that the rebels had any hope of being able to resist the attack of our forces. The surrender of the

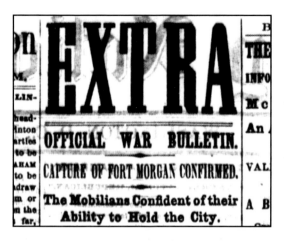

Left: "Capture of Fort Morgan Confirmed." *From the* National Republican, *August 29, 1864.*

Below: "Fort Morgan, Alabama. Ruins of Fort…View of Citadel looking South East." Note that the Citadel no longer exists— only foundations remain. *Courtesy of the Library of Congress.*

fort as you will learn from other sources took place on the 28d. An officer recently from the field of operations, describes the prospect of the early capture of Mobile as extremely encouraging. The confidence of the officers of the naval and land forces is complete.…

…The War Department has just received Gen. Canby's official report of the surrender of Fort Morgan, Mobile, Aug. 24.

Fort Morgan surrendered unconditionally yesterday at 2 p.m. We have about 500 prisoners, 60 pieces of artillery and a large quantity of material.

In the 12 hours proceeding the surrender, about 3000 shells were thrown into the Fort. The buildings and barracks were entirely destroyed and the works generally much injured; many guns were spiked, carriages burned and much ammunition destroyed by the rebels.

The loss of our army were 1 killed and 7 wounded.

Signed R.S. Canby, Maj. Gen.[77]

In 1895, the U.S. Army Corps of Engineers began upgrading Fort Morgan with concrete batteries instead of brick. From 1900 to 1923, there was a garrison of four hundred Coast Artillery soldiers stationed there. During World War I, up to two thousand troops were stationed at Fort Morgan.

During World War II, the U.S. Navy took over the fort. In April 1942, the 50th Coast Artillery Regiment was stationed at Morgan. The fort was finally abandoned in July 1944.

Date	Event(s)
1813	Fort Bowyer is constructed where Fort Morgan exists today.
September 15, 1814	Battle of Fort Bowyer is an American victory against the British and a number of Creek Indians.
February 1815	Second Battle of Fort Bowyer is a British victory, but the Treaty of Ghent specifies that the fort be returned to the Americans.
1819	The U.S. Army Corps of Engineers begins construction on Fort Morgan.
1833–34	Fort Morgan (masonry) is completed and named in honor of Revolutionary War hero General Daniel Morgan.
1836–37	Fort Morgan is a stop on the Trail of Tears.
1842	Fort Morgan is put into inactive status.
January 4, 1861	Fort Morgan is seized by troops from Alabama.

Date	Event(s)
March 1861	Confederate army takes control of the fort.
April 30, 1863	Fort commander Lieutenant Colonel C. Stewart is killed in a cannon explosion.
August 5, 1864	Battle of Mobile Bay.
August 22, 1864	Union bombardment of Fort Morgan begins.
August 23, 1864	Brigadier General Richard L. Page surrenders Fort Morgan after his magazines are threatened by Union bombardment—581 men surrender, and 17 were killed in the bombardment.
1895	U.S. Army Corps of Engineers begins upgrading Fort Morgan with concrete batteries instead of brick.
1900–1923	Garrison of four hundred Coast Artillery soldiers.
1906, 1916	Hurricane damage to the fort.
World War I	Up to two thousand troops are stationed at Fort Morgan.
1923	Once again, the fort is returned to inactive status.
November 1941	U.S. Navy takes over the fort.
April 1942	50th Coast Guard Artillery Regiment is stationed at Morgan.
July 1944	Fort Morgan is abandoned.
December 19, 1960	Fort Morgan becomes a National Historic Landmark.
October 15, 1966	Fort Morgan added to the National Register of Historic Places.
2007	Listed as "one of the nation's 10 most endangered battle sites" by the Civil War Preservation Trust.

WHAT IS LEFT TO SEE

- Fort Blakeley (34745 State Highway 225, Spanish Fort, AL, 36577)
- Fort Gaines (51 Bienville Boulevard, Dauphin Island, AL, 36528)
- Fort McDermott ("Fort McDermott is in the south end of Spanish Fort, just above US Highway 31 bounded by Confederate Drive, Spanish Main Street, Rebel Road, and Cannonade Drive."[78] There are several parking spaces at the intersection of Cannonade Boulevard and Spanish Main Street.)
- Fort Morgan (51 Highway 180 West, Gulf Shores, AL, 36542)

Notes

INTRODUCTION

1. *Birmingham Historical Society Newsletter* (March/April 2015).
2. National Park Service, U.S. Department of the Interior, "Update to the Civil War Sites, Advisory Commission Report on the Nation's Civil War Battlefields," http://www.nps.gov/abpp/CWSII/CWSACReportAlabamaUpdate.pdf.

CHAPTER 1

3. Jordan, *Campaigns of Lieut.-Gen. N.B. Forrest*.
4. Ibid.
5. Whipple, *Memorial Service Held in Honor*.
6. Civil War Artillery Projectiles, "The Civil War Diary of General Josiah Gorgas," http://www.civilwarartillery.com/books/jgorgas1.pdf.
7. Ibid.
8. Ibid.
9. Beers, *Memories*.
10. *Confederate Military History*.
11. Alabama Department of Archives and History, "Excerpts from the Diary of a Confederate Soldier, by John Washington Inzer," http://digital.archives.alabama.gov/cdm/ref/collection/voices/id/1799.

12. Jones, *Captain Roger Jones*.
13. In his name, "ap" is Welsh for "son of."
14. *War of the Rebellion*, series 1, vol. 21.
15. Brock, *Southern Historical Society Papers*, 37.
16. *War of the Rebellion*, series 1, vol. 21.
17. Moore, *Voices of the Heart*.
18. *Anderson Intelligencer*, August 28, 1901.
19. Some sources say "Philip."
20. Some sources say 1826.
21. Evans, *Alabama*, vol. 7, *Confederate Military History*.
22. Some sources say "Emmet."
23. *War of the Rebellion*, series 1, vol. 27.
24. *Joe Mitchell Chapple's National Magazine* 40.
25. Wyeth, *Life of General Nathan Bedford Forrest*.
26. Semmes, *Memoirs of Service Afloat*.
27. Ibid.
28. Dodson, *Campaigns of Wheeler and His Cavalry*.
29. *Raftsman's Journal*, May 3, 1865.
30. Bartleby, "His Speech of Protest in the Charleston Convention: William Lowndes Yancey (1814–63)," http://www.bartleby.com/268/9/19.html.
31. The group included William Barksdale, James Dunwoody Brownson DeBow, Thomas C. Hindman, Laurence M. Keitt, William Porcher Miles, John A. Quitman, Robert Rhett, Edmund Ruffin, Nathaniel Beverley Tucker, Louis Wigfall and William Lowndes Yancey.

CHAPTER 3

32. Cory, *Ladies' Memorial Association of Montgomery*.
33. Chesnut, *Diary from Dixie*.

CHAPTER 4

34. *War of the Rebellion*, series 1, vol. 21.
35. Headley, *Old Stars*.
36. *Yorkville Enquirer*, April 24, 1862.
37. *Highland Weekly News*, April 24, 1862.
38. Pun intended.

39. Wikipedia, "Report of Col. Abel D. Streight, August 2, 1864," http://en.wikisource.org/wiki/Report_of_Col._Abel_D._Streight,_August_22,_1864.
40. Ibid.
41. Ibid.
42. Dixon, *Naval History of the Civil War*.
43. The American Battlefield Protection Program (ABPP), "Mobile Bay," CWSAC Battle Summaries, www.nps.gov/abpp/battles/al003.htm.
44. Dixon, *Naval History of the Civil War*.
45. Farragut, *Life of David Glasgow Farragut*.
46. *War of the Rebellion*, series 2, vol. 1.
47. Ibid.
48. The part of the bow or stem that "cuts through the water."
49. Dixon, *Naval History of the Civil War*.
50. *War of the Rebellion*, series 1, vol. 21.
51. Ibid., vol. 49, part 1.
52. *Tri-Weekly Herald*, April 15, 1865.
53. *Evening Star*, May 4, 1865.
54. *War of the Rebellion*, series 1, vol. 49, part 1.
55. *Nashville Daily Union*, May 4, 1865.
56. Other sources suggest that the number defending the fort was closer to 120.
57. *Memphis Daily Appeal*, December 27, 1865.
58. Ibid.
59. *War of the Rebellion*, series 1, vol. 21.
60. *Birmingham Historical Society Newsletter* (March/April 2015).
61. *War of the Rebellion*, series 1, vol. 49, part 1.
62. Ibid.
63. Ibid.
64. Taylor, *Destruction and Reconstruction*.
65. Ibid.
66. Ibid.

Chapter 5

67. Civil War Artillery Projectiles, "Civil War Diary of General Josiah Gorgas."
68. *War of the Rebellion*, series 1, vol. 49, part 1.
69. "The section of a blast furnace between the hearth and the stack, having the form of a frustum of an inverted cone." http://dictionary.reference.com/browse/bosh.

70. *War of the Rebellion*, series 1, vol. 49, part 1.

71. National Park Service, U.S. Department of the Interior, "National Register of Historic Places Inventory—Nomination Form: Confederate Armory Site," https://www.apps.mdah.ms.gov/nom/prop/22177.pdf.

72. *War of the Rebellion*, series 1, vol. 49, part 1.

73. Gorgas, *Journals of Josiah Gorgas*.

74. *Birmingham Historical Society Newsletter* (March/April 2015).

CHAPTER 7

75. *War of the Rebellion*, series 1, vol. 39, part 1.

76. Ibid.

77. *Daily Intelligencer*, September 2, 1864.

78. Admiral Raphael Semmes Camp #11, "Fort McDermott Maps," http://www.scvsemmes.org/fort-mcdermott-maps.html.

Sources

Anderson Intelligencer. August 28, 1901.

Beers, Fannie A. *Memories: A Record of Personal Experience and Adventure During Four Years of War.* Philadelphia, PA: J.B. Lippincott Company, 1888.

Birmingham Historical Society Newsletter (March–April 2015).

Brock, R.A. *Southern Historical Society Papers* 37 (1909).

Chesnut, Mary Boykin Miller. *A Diary from Dixie.* New York: D. Appleton and Company, 1905.

Cleveland Morning Leader. April 13, 1865.

Confederate Military History: A Library of Confederate States History. Atlanta, GA: Confederate Publishing Company, 1899.

Cory, Marielou Armstrong, comp. *Ladies' Memorial Association of Montgomery, Alabama.* Montgomery: Alabama Printing Company, 1902.

Daily Intelligencer. September 2, 1864.

Dodson, W.C., ed. *Campaigns of Wheeler and His Cavalry, 1862–1865.* Atlanta, GA: Hudgins Publishing Company, 1899.

Evans, General Clement, ed. *Confederate Military History.* Vol. 7, *Alabama.* Atlanta, GA: Confederate Publishing Company, 1899.

Evening Star. May 4, 1865.

Farragut, Loyall. *The Life of David Glasgow Farragut, First Admiral of the United States Navy.* New York: D. Appleton and Company, 1891.

Gorgas, Josiah. *The Journals of Josiah Gorgas, 1857–1878.* Tuscaloosa: University of Alabama Press, 1995.

Headley, Phineas Camp. *Old Stars: The Life and Military Career of Major-General Ormsby M. Mitchel.* Boston: Lee & Shepard, 1883.

Highland Weekly News. April 24, 1862.

Inzer, John Washington. *Diary of a Confederate Soldier.* Edited by Mattie Lou Teague Crow. Madison: University of Wisconsin–Madison, Strode Publishers, 1977.

Joe Mitchell Chapple's National Magazine 40 (1914). Chapple Publishing Company.

Jones, Lewis Hampton. *Captain Roger Jones, of London and Virginia: Some of His Antecedents and Descendants.* Albany, NY: Joel Munsell's Sons, 1891.

Jordan, Thomas, and J.P. Pryor. *Campaigns of Lieut.-Gen. N.B. Forrest, and of Forrest's Cavalry.* New Orleans, LA: Blelock & Company, 1868.

Memphis Daily Appeal. December 27, 1865.

Montana Post. May 20, 1865.

Moore, Cordelia Elizabeth. *Voices of the Heart: A Book of Poems.* Louisville, KY, 1914.

Nashville Daily Union. May 4, 1865.

Nashville Union. April 21, 1865.

Nashville Union and American. September 30, 1870.

National Republican. August 29, 1864.

New-York Daily Tribune. April 26, 1865.

The Official Records of the Union and Confederate Navies in the War of the Rebellion. Series 2, vol. 1. Naval War Records Office. Washington, D.C.: Government Printing Office, 1921.

Porter, David Dixon. *The Naval History of the Civil War.* New York: Sherman Publishing Company, 1886.

Raftsman's Journal. May 3, 1865.

Semmes, Raphael. *Memoirs of Service Afloat: During the War Between the States.* Baltimore, MD: Kelly, Piet and Company, 1869.

Taylor, Richard. *Destruction and Reconstruction: Personal Experiences of the Late War.* Edinburgh: William Blackwood & Sons, 1874.

Tri-Weekly Herald. April 15, 1865.

The War of the Rebellion: A Compilation of the Official Records of the Union and Confederate Armies. Series 1, vols. 21, 27, 39 and 49. Washington, D.C.: Government Printing Office, 1888, 1888, 1892 and 1897.

Whipple, Mary Rayner. *Memorial Service Held in Honor of Major General William Crawford Gorgas.* Southern Society of Washington, D.C., 1921.

Wyeth, Dr. John A. *Life of General Nathan Bedford Forrest.* New York: Harper & Brother, Publishers, 1908.

Yancey, William. *His Speech of Protest in the Charleston Convention.* 1860.

Yorkville Enquirer. April 24, 1862.

LINKS

http://dictionary.reference.com/browse/bosh.

http://digital.archives.alabama.gov/cdm/ref/collection/voices/id/1799.

http://en.wikisource.org/wiki/Report_of_Col._Abel_D._Streight,_August_22,_1864.

http://www.bartleby.com/268/9/19.html.

http://www.civilwarartillery.com/books/jgorgas1.pdf.

http://www.conventiontradecenter.com/history.cfm.

http://www.cr.nps.gov/hps/abpp/battles/al003.htm.

http://www.nps.gov/abpp/CWSII/CWSACReportAlabamaUpdate.pdf.

https://www.apps.mdah.ms.gov/nom/prop/22177.pdf.

Library of Congress. http://hdl.loc.gov/loc.gmd/g3866sm.gcw0102000.

———. http://hdl.loc.gov/loc.gmd/g3924c.cws00065.

———. http://hdl.loc.gov/loc.gmd/g3970.rr001780.

———. http://hdl.loc.gov/loc.gmd/g3974s.cw0112000.

———. http://hdl.loc.gov/loc.ndlpcoop/gvhs01.vhs00200.

———. http://hdl.loc.gov/loc.ndlpcoop/gvhs01.vhs00201.

———. http://www.loc.gov/pictures/item/2001704280.

———. http://www.loc.gov/pictures/item/2002712784.

———. http://www.loc.gov/pictures/item/2003663830.

———. http://www.loc.gov/pictures/item/2004660809.

———. http://www.loc.gov/pictures/item/2010637553.

———. http://www.loc.gov/pictures/item/2012647345.

———. http://www.loc.gov/pictures/item/2012649979.

———. http://www.loc.gov/pictures/item/2012650203.

———. http://www.loc.gov/pictures/item/2013646182.

———. http://www.loc.gov/pictures/item/2013647475.

———. http://www.loc.gov/pictures/item/2014646255.

———. http://www.loc.gov/pictures/item/93510337.

———. http://www.loc.gov/pictures/item/95505193.

———. http://www.loc.gov/pictures/item/al0276.photos.003242p.

———. http://www.loc.gov/pictures/item/al0643.photos.005875p.

———. http://www.loc.gov/pictures/item/al0646.photos.005941p.

———. http://www.loc.gov/pictures/item/brh2009000003/PP.

———. http://www.loc.gov/pictures/item/cwp2003000359/PP.

———. http://www.loc.gov/pictures/item/cwp2003000406/PP.

———. http://www.loc.gov/pictures/item/cwp2003000446/PP.

———. http://www.loc.gov/pictures/item/cwp2003002570/PP.

————. http://www.loc.gov/pictures/item/cwp2003004903/PP.
————. http://www.loc.gov/pictures/item/det1994001180/PP.
————. http://www.loc.gov/pictures/item/det1994014627/PP.
————. http://www.loc.gov/pictures/item/fl0021.photos.052350p.
www.wikimedia.org.
www.wikipedia.org.

The Author on YouTube

There are several extracts of lectures by the author on Civil War topics available on YouTube.

Author singing "Hold the Fort." http://www.youtube.com/watch?v=5LzWtVXAYAE.

"A Brief Look at 'Bloody Bill' Anderson." http://youtu.be/Y-vA6BKaOWA.

"A Brief Look at Patrick Cleburne." http://youtu.be/qagsf7uUgZo.

"Civil War Quick Note: Clara Barton." http://youtu.be/7Td0lu49hsw.

"Overview of the Great Locomotive Chase." http://www.youtube.com/watch?v=CSJ03W8mlMc.

"Sherman's March: Strategy and Results." http://www.youtube.com/watch?v=gAcqx0rpWXY.

"Sherman's March: The Fall of Savannah." http://www.youtube.com/watch?v=Iykjb7vA3wI.

Index

About the Author

R obert C. Jones served as president of the Kennesaw Historical Society for twenty-one years (1994–2015) and also served as a member of the executive board of the Kennesaw Museum Foundation for seventeen years (1998–2015). The Museum Foundation helped fund the forty-five-thousand-square-foot Southern Museum of Civil War and Locomotive History in Kennesaw, Georgia. He has written more than forty books on historical themes, including several books on "Old West" themes.

Robert C. Jones is an ordained elder in the Presbyterian Church. He has written and taught numerous adult Sunday school courses. He is also the author of a number of books on Christian history and theology topics (for a list, see http:// rcjbooks.com/christian_history).

In 2005, Robert coauthored a business-oriented book, *Working Virtually: The Challenges of Virtual Teams*. In 2013, Robert authored a book on World War I titled *The Top 10 Innovations of World War I* and published *The Leo Beuerman Story: As Told by His Family*. In 2014, Robert published *Ghost Towns and Mills of the Atlanta Area*. In 2016, he published *The Top Innovations of World War II*.

The author is available for lectures in Georgia, Alabama, southern Tennessee, eastern Kansas and southeastern Pennsylvania. For details, see http://www. rcjbooks.com/guest_speaker.

OTHER WORKS BY THE AUTHOR

HISTORICAL BOOKS:

The Battle of Allatoona Pass: The Forgotten Battle of Sherman's Atlanta Campaign

The Battle of Chickamauga: A Brief History

The Battle of Griswoldville: An Infantry Battle on Sherman's March to the Sea

Bleeding Kansas: The Real Start of the Civil War

Civil War Prison Camps: A Brief History

Colonial Georgia: 1733–1800

The Confederate Invasion of New Mexico

Conspirators, Assassins, and the Death of Abraham Lincoln

The End of the Civil War: 1865

The End of the Civil War in Georgia: 1865

Famous Songs of the Civil War

The Fifteen Most Critical Moments of the Civil War

George Washington and the Continental Army: 1777–1778

Great Naval Battles of the Civil War

A Guide to the Civil War in Alabama

A Guide to the Civil War in Georgia

Heroes and Heroines of the American Revolution

Lost Confederate Gold

McCook's Raid and the Battle of Brown's Mill

The Pennsylvania Railroad: An Illustrated Timeline

The Reading Railroad: An Illustrated Timeline

Retracing the Route of Sherman's Atlanta Campaign (expanded edition)

Retracing the Route of Sherman's March to the Sea (expanded edition)

The Ten Best—and Worst—Generals of the Civil War

The Top 10 Reasons Why the Civil War Was Won in the West

The Top 20 Civil War Spies and Secret Agents

The Top 20 Railroad Songs of All Time

The Top 25 Most Influential Women of the Civil War

The W&A, the General, and the Andrews Raid: A Brief History

The War of 1812: A Brief History

"OLD WEST" BOOKS:

Death Valley Ghost Towns—As They Appear Today

Ghost Towns, Forts and Pueblos of New Mexico (expanded edition)

Ghost Towns of Southern Arizona and New Mexico

Ghost Towns of the Mojave National Preserve

Ghost Towns of Western Nevada

A Guide to Frontier Kansas

The Top 10 Gunslingers and Lawmen of the Old West